Sewing Dolls

Sewing Dolls

Karin Neuschütz

in collaboration with Kerstin Rehnman

Floris Books

Translated by Susan Beard
Photographs by Thomas Wingstedt and Karin Neuschütz
Illustrations by Kerstin Rehnman

First published in Swedish as *Sy mjuka dockor*
by Forma Publishing Group AB in 2009
First published in English by Floris Books in 2009

British Library CIP data available

ISBN 978-086315-719-6

Printed in Singapore

Contents

Foreword

When I first became a mother over thirty years ago I learnt to make soft dolls like the ones made in Waldorf schools. From my workshop I produced one doll character after the other, and it wasn't long before I had written and printed a booklet on the art of making soft dolls. Towards the end of the 1970s a publisher saw the booklet and asked me if I would write a book about children's play and dolls, and that's what I did. Since then a long list of books has followed — so I can thank the dolls for making me an author.

Soon the soft dolls were given the name Waldorf dolls, and the art of sewing them has spread throughout Sweden and Europe and into the world. I sometimes receive photographs of dolls with greetings from all around Europe, Hawaii, South Africa, Korea and Japan. I have taught many courses on sewing dolls over the years too.

When one of my doll books went out of print I was commissioned to write a new one. In the autumn of 2006 I concentrated on producing a series of dolls from new patterns and with new methods of shaping the bodies and heads. I entered into a very rewarding collaboration with Kerstin Rehnman, who has designed all the clothes patterns and sewn the clothes for the dolls in this book. She has enjoyed doll-making since 1998 and she makes delightful porcelain, papier mâché and Glorex dolls in historical costumes.

Our aim is to make the clothes, as well as the dolls, easy to sew and use. We hope this book inspires many adults and children to take out a needle and thread and start sewing dolls.

Karen Neuschütz

Introduction

A doll can be a good friend, who always listens and helps the child formulate their feelings and thoughts. Children act out different roles when they're playing with dolls: what it's like to be an adult, to be a mother or father, or another child. With the doll's help the child can work through past experiences and gain perspective.

The doll is an image of a human being; throughout time such images have always had a special ability to engage us.

The most important thing about a Waldorf doll is its simple face, which allows the child to freely invent the doll's personality and feelings without their imagination being limited by clearly defined features. The doll can take on new characteristics and grow with the child, and it's always soft and huggable. There are no other rules about the look of a Waldorf doll; it can be made from an old sock, a mitten or from fine cotton knit. In a Waldorf school, children in Class Six craft lessons design and sew their own doll when they begin

learning about human biology. The doll is made from natural materials: cotton fabrics, wool and woollen yarns.

The simplest doll you can make is created by knotting a handkerchief. Place a small ball of sheep's wool near one corner of a handkerchief (figure 1). Fold the corner over the ball, wind a length of yarn around the neck and tie (figure 2). Draw or sew dots for the eyes and mouth. Make a knot in two corners of the handkerchief for hands. The rest of the head corner can be turned back to form a hood (figure 3).

Even quite small children can make a doll like this, draw on its face and sew on some strands of hair. It's easy to learn how, and the doll can be developed as the child's confidence in sewing and making knots grows. Sense of colour and a feeling for style and materials all develop as the child works with fabric and wool, making dolls' clothes and accessories.

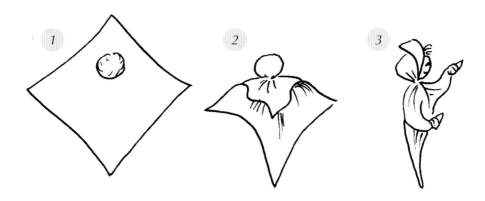

Children appreciate it when adults show an interest in their toys. If we help to care for the doll, to hug it and tuck it up in bed, the child feels reassured that they are doing the right thing in their play. Importantly, a doll can also inspire creative 'chatty' play.

You might find, while you are sewing, that you become quite attached to a doll. Why not make another one to give away! Dolls are not only for children: many adults collect these beautifully crafted objects.

The patterns in this book, for both dolls and clothes, are all new, and several new ways of forming the stuffed dolls, such as using a felting needle, are suggested.

The first dolls in the book are simple — small models suitable for young children. Then come two different types of larger dressing-up dolls and patterns for their clothes. Finally there are two smaller models with moveable arms and legs, which are fun for slightly older children who can make a whole wardrobe of clothes for their doll by themselves.

If there's one particular doll that can be called a 'Waldorf doll' it's this simple knotted doll made from a handkerchief. You can make the quilt as follows: cut cotton material for the top and a piece of wadding or blanket to measure 32 x 40 cm (12 1/2 in x 15 3/4 in), and a bottom piece to measure 49 x 57 cm (19 1/4 x 22 1/2 in). Lay the upper piece on top of the wadding with the right side facing up and sew them together in a squared pattern. Lay the bottom piece of material underneath with the reverse facing upwards. Fold the edges of the bottom piece over the upper piece, pin and then sew the edging in place.

Getting Started

Sewing

A solid line indicates the cutting line in all the patterns in this book.

Inside the solid line is a dotted line, which indicates where you are to sew. Between them is a seam allowance of approximately 0.5 cm (¹/4 in).

The broken lines with longer dashes indicate where the fabric is folded double.

Lines made up of dots and dashes mean that the actual pattern is folded or must be extended at that point, due to lack of room on the page in the book. When you trace it, be sure to extend that part.

Double dotted lines indicate gathering: sew two straight seams with a long stitch length on your machine, take hold of the threads of each seam and pull them both at the same time.

Horizontal lines drawn in the seam allowance indicate that small nicks must be cut in the fabric to make it easier to turn the work.

Sewing tips

- Make sure you put a new needle in the machine; a damaged needle can make a hole in cotton knit. A ball-point needle is best.
- Zigzag the edges of all pieces before sewing them together if the material is fraying.
- When sewing velour, pin and tack all pieces together before you sew, or the material will stretch.

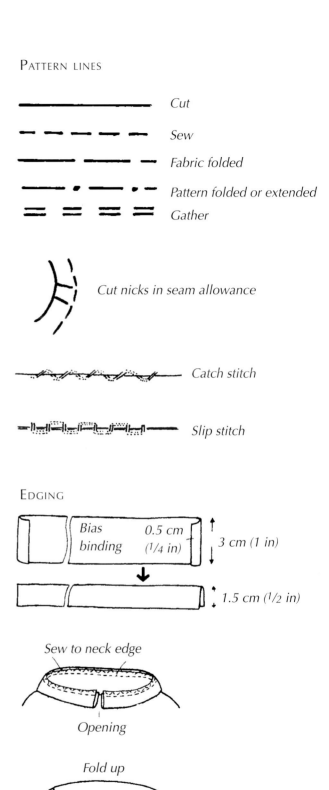

Pattern lines

Cut

Sew

Fabric folded

Pattern folded or extended

Gather

Cut nicks in seam allowance

Catch stitch

Slip stitch

Edging

Bias binding   0.5 cm (¹/4 in)   3 cm (1 in)

1.5 cm (¹/2 in)

Sew to neck edge

Opening

Fold up

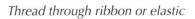

Thread through ribbon or elastic

- With thin cotton-knit fabric, it's easiest to draw the pieces on the fabric and sew them before you cut them out. Sew using a stretch setting or a narrow zigzag.
- When the edges are sewn by hand use catch stitch or slip stitch (see diagram on the previous page).
- Always try the clothes on your own doll before you sew them.
- Sew cuffs and edgings as shown in the diagram.
- It can be difficult to thread elastic in a small sleeve. You will find it easier if you spread the sleeve out flat before sewing it together, thread the elastic through, stitch one end of the elastic to one side, pull the elastic taut, stitch the other end of the elastic and then sew the sleeve together.
- The clothes patterns have brief descriptions; we assume you know that the seams are sewn with right sides facing!

Materials

Both the dolls and their clothes are best if made from natural materials. The different doll models are made from flesh-coloured, stretchy cotton knit, with one exception: models Tim and Tina are made from stiff cotton fabric. Look in your cupboards at home — perhaps you have odd pieces of material that can be turned into dolls or clothes? Choose thinner fabric for the dolls clothes.

The dolls are stuffed with washed, carded sheep's wool, known as 'stuffing wool.' One tightly squeezed fistful is the equivalent of about 10 grams ($1/3$ oz). For each model the amount of materials needed is given.

You will be able to buy wool, cotton knit, rug warp and gauze tubing in craft shops. You can also buy gauze tubing at the pharmacy.

If the recipient of the doll is allergic to wool, the doll can be stuffed with cotton waste or synthetic wadding (ask in a fabric shop).

TOOLS
- Sewing machine, preferably with stretch seam, or at least zigzag
- A good pair of fabric scissors
- A long darning needle, at least 7 cm (2 $3/4$ in)
- Pins
- Needles and thread
- Pliers can be helpful when pulling the darning needle through the doll
- A soft pencil to copy the patterns and mark the fabric
- Chopsticks or other bamboo sticks for stuffing
- A 1–2 cm ($1/3$–$3/4$ in) wide and 30 cm (12 in) long strip cut from thin plastic, or equivalent size satin ribbon, to help insert the large dolls' limbs
- A felting needle to help you to sculpt the stuffing wool

Washing the dolls

The dolls can be washed by hand with soap, lukewarm water and a soft sponge. Rinse under running warm water. After washing, squeeze them in a towel and leave to dry in an airy place.

The dolls' clothes should also be hand washed, especially if they are sewn or knitted in a delicate fibre such as wool. Cotton clothes can be washed in a machine on a delicate cycle. It's fun for children to take part in the washing. You might be able to get hold of mini clothes pegs and hang the clothes on a string at child height.

Angel / Baggy Doll

Make a soft angel to hang over the crib or pram. Without her wings and hair band she can be a sweet little baggy doll to cuddle in bed. She is 15 cm (6 in) tall.

MATERIALS

- Thin skin-coloured cotton knit: 5 x10 cm (2 x 4 in) for the head and body; two pieces 2 x 6 cm (3/4 in x 2 1/3 in) for the hands and feet
- For the dress: two pieces of velour or felt, each 12 x 12 cm (4 3/4 x 4 3/4 in)
- For the wings: two pieces of white felt, velour or sheeting, each 9 x 9 cm (3 1/2 x 3 1/2 in)
- About 10g (1/3 oz) stuffing wool
- Some thin-ply wool, silk roving or carded wool for the hair
- 10 cm (4 in) elastic or cotton ribbon for hanging up the angel
- Thin gold thread for the hair band and sewing thread for the eyes and mouth

1. For the head and body, fold the cotton-knit fabric double lengthwise along the ribbing. Knot the elastic to form a loop. Place the loop into the fabric at the head end (figure 1, p15), with the knot on the outside. Sew along the line, trim the corner and turn the bag the right way out so that the loop is on the outside (figure 2).
2. Wind some wool stuffing into a ball (about the size of a grape) and push it down into the bottom of the bag. Tie a thread around the neck. Fill the rest of the bag fairly loosely; that will become the body. Sew together at the base (figure 3).
3. Cut out two small hands and two small feet from the remnants of the cotton knit using the pattern and sew (figure 4). Trim the edges and turn the right way out.
4. Trace and cut out the dress pattern. Lay it on double fabric, draw round the templates and cut out a back and a front piece. Place the pieces right sides together, pinning at the centre to keep them in place. Insert the hands in the cuffs and the feet at the bottom, turned the right way out, so that they point inwards

and lie between the front and back dress pieces (figure 5). Pin in place.

5. Stitch along the dotted line around the whole dress apart from the neck, and leave an opening in the side (figure 5). Sew in the hands and feet at the same time. Turn the whole thing right side out.

6. Insert the body through the neck opening, turn the head seam to the back and sew securely around the dress neck opening. Stuff a little wool into the arms and the bottom of the dress. Sew up the opening in the side of the dress.

ANGEL / BAGGY DOLL

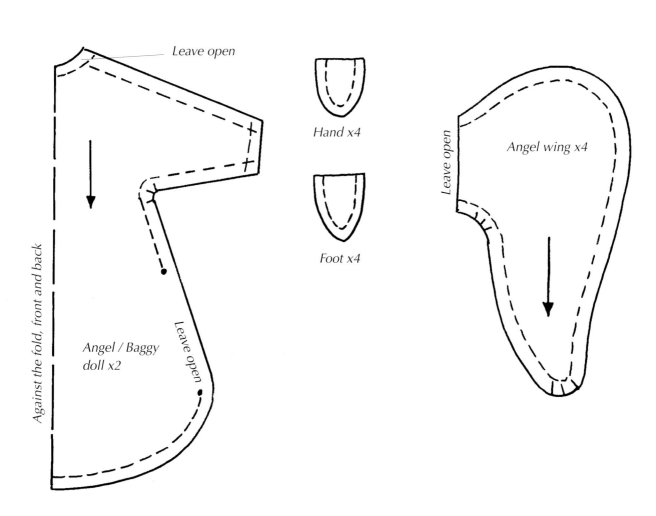

Leave open

Hand x4

Foot x4

Leave open

Angel wing x4

Against the fold, front and back

Angel / Baggy doll x2

Leave open

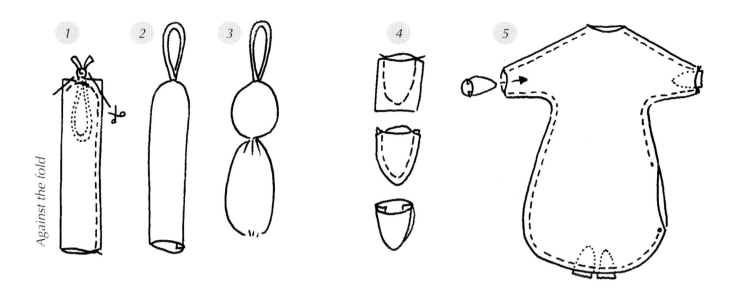

Against the fold

The soft little Baggy Doll in pink velour is sitting and dreaming as the angel floats by whispering secrets in her ear. The same pattern is used for both dolls.

7. Lay the hair right across the crown of the head in front of and behind the loop and stitch a middle parting (figure 6).

8. Sew a seam around the nape of the neck (figure 7). Put a gold band in the hair, if required.

9. Place the wing pattern on to double white fabric, right sides facing. Sew round the wings leaving an opening for turning. Trim the wings and turn them right side out. If the wings are limp they can be stiffened by sewing rows of straight seams across them. Sew up the opening (the wings are not stuffed) as you stitch the wings to the angel's back, so that they extend above the shoulders.

10. Sew small, faint dots for the eyes and mouth.

Softy

A cuddly little velour elf, a sweet little mascot or a perfect present for a baby. Little Softy, the smaller sized doll, is about 10 cm (4 in) tall, and Big Softy, the larger one, about 20 cm (8 in). See the photographs on pages 19, 46 and 76.

MATERIALS (BIG SOFTY)
- Velour in a bright colour: 20 x 15 cm (40 x 30 cm)/ 8 x 6 in (15 3/4 x 11 3/4 in)
- Flesh-coloured cotton knit for the head and hands: 10 x 5 cm (20 x 8 cm)/ 4 x 2 in (8 x 3 in)
- Wool for stuffing: 5g (30g)/ 1/6 oz (1 oz)
- Small amount of wool or yarn for the hair and sewing thread for the eyes and mouth
- A stick for turning the material and for stuffing
- A felting needle and a sponge as a base (if required)

1. Trace the pattern pieces (pages 20–21), cut them out and lay them on the wrong side of the material with the arrows following the grain of the fabric. The sides should be facing different directions (figure 1). Draw round the pattern pieces on the material and cut them out.
2. If using velour it's important to tack first, otherwise the pieces shift. Place the side pieces right sides together and tack them from A to B (figure 2).
3. Sew using stretch seam on a machine or by hand using backstitch, following the dotted line. Spread out the arms and legs and lay the front piece on top, right sides facing. Pin, tack and sew all round, leaving openings for the hands and head (figure 3).

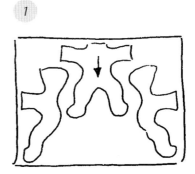

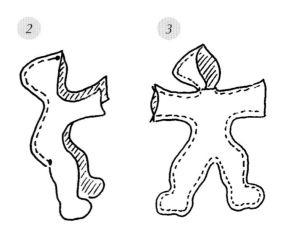

Place the pattern pieces like this on the fabric

4. Fold the head cotton knit double along the ribbing. Sew a seam as shown on the pattern. Cut halfway up the fold and turn right side out.

5. Wind wool into a small ball with a circumference of 8 cm (15 cm)/ 3 in (6 in) for the head (figure 4).

6. It might be helpful to shape the head using a felting needle, resting the head on a sponge (figure 5).

7. Stuff the head ball into the head fabric, making sure the seam is at the back, and tie round the neck.

8. Take two small wads of wool and tie them in place with sewing thread to form a round hand at each end of the fabric hanging below the head (figure 7).

9. Fill the doll's feet, legs and body with wool. Avoid stuffing where the legs join the body,

to make it easier for the doll to sit. Using the stick, push one hand into each arm and position the head so that the arms are filled with the head fabric (figure 8).

10. Sew a row of gathering stitches round the neck, turn in the seam allowance, pull tightly and sew the front piece to the throat.

11. Push in a piece of hair yarn or wool between the hood and the head, or make plaits with some longer strands (figure 9).

12. Turn under the seam allowance and attach the hood neatly, sewing the hair in place at the same time. Stitch dots on the face for features. Turn in the hem allowance on the sleeves and stitch to the hands.

The pattern for this happy little pixie, feeding her horse with hay, is on pages 20–21. There is also a pattern for a smaller Softy doll.

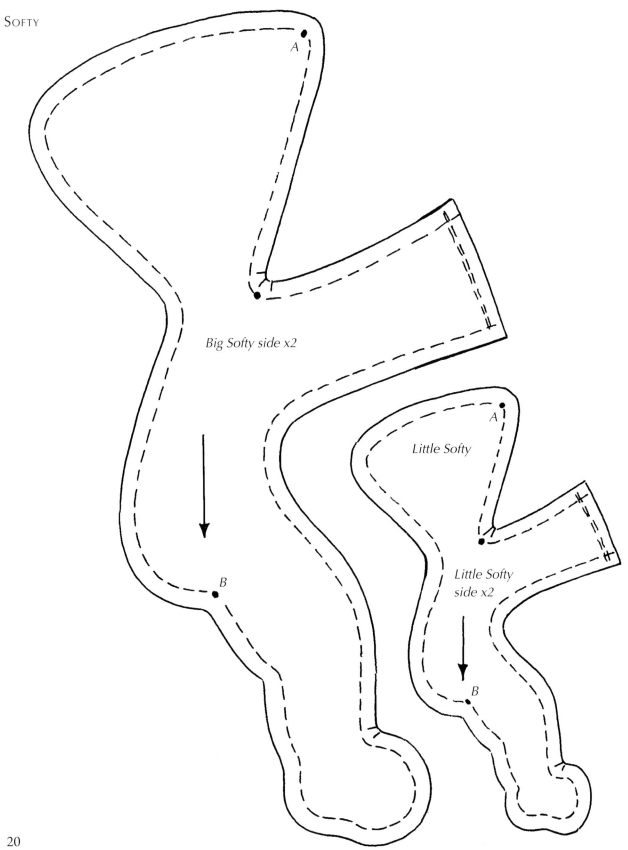

Big Softy side x2

A

B

Little Softy

A

Little Softy
side x2

B

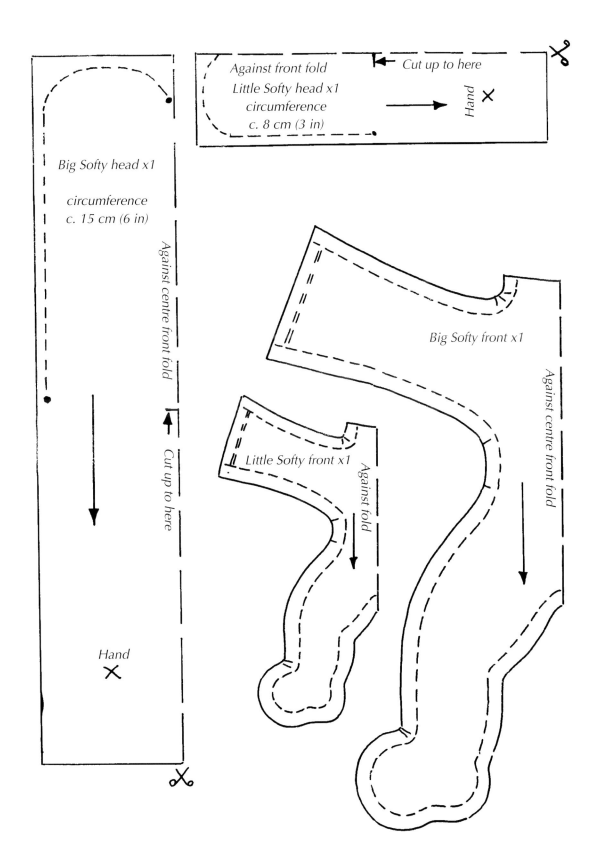

Big Softy head x1

circumference
c. 15 cm (6 in)

Against centre front fold

Cut up to here

Hand
X

Against front fold
Little Softy head x1
circumference
c. 8 cm (3 in)

Cut up to here

Hand
X

Big Softy front x1

Against centre front fold

Little Softy front x1

Against fold

Sonia & Sam

A cuddly, knitted doll for very small children that's simple to make. The body is knitted in garter stitch in two pieces, and the finished doll is 15–20 cm (6–8 in) tall, depending on wool thickness.

MATERIALS
- A small ball of wool or cotton yarn in a bright colour
- Needles size 2–3 (mm)/ 14–11 (UK) / 0–2 (US)
- A small piece of flesh-coloured cotton-knit fabric and an oddment of wool or yarn for the hair
- 10–20 g ($^1/_3$–$^3/_4$ oz) of stuffing wool
- Sewing thread for the eyes and mouth and to attach the hair

1. Cast on 30 stitches (s) for the top piece. Knit 10 rows (r) plain. Divide the piece in two by knitting 15s for a further 10r, then casting off. Knit the remaining 15 stitches for 10r and then cast off (figure 1, p. 24).
2. Cast on 20s for the lower section and knit 25r in garter stitch. Cast off 13s then knit to the end of the row (7s). Turn, knit the 7s and then cast on 13 new stitches (by making loose half loops round the needle). Continue to knit 25 rows and then cast off (figure 2).
3. Sew the legs together at the bottom and all the way up to the crotch. Sew the centre back seam of the lower section. Sew the seams under the arms, measuring against the lower section to see how longs the arms should be (figure 3).
4. Sew the lower and upper sections together at the waist (figure 4).
5. Make the head according to the instructions for Softy on pages 17–18. Adapt the size of the head to your knitting. The head can be slightly more than half the body's length (figure 5).

You can quickly knit a sweet little doll from squares of garter stitch in wool or cotton. Meet Sonia and Sam, who love playing in the garden.

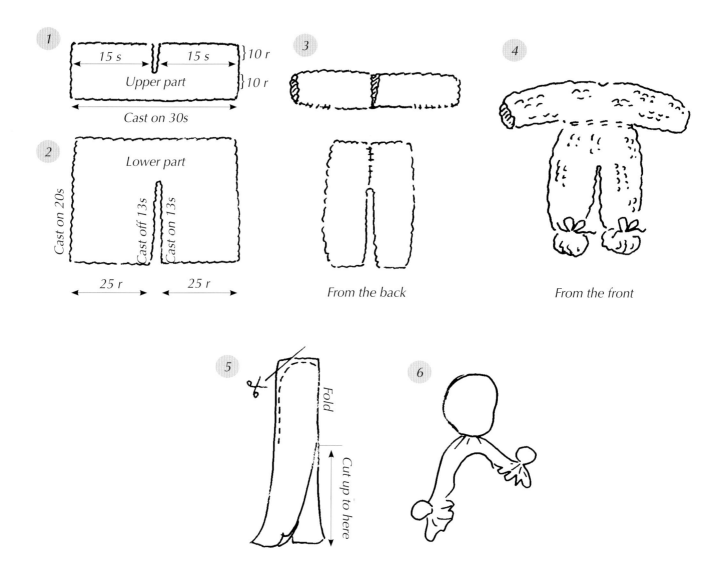

1

15 s   15 s   } 10 r

Upper part   } 10 r

Cast on 30s

2

Lower part

Cast on 20s

Cast off 13s

Cast on 13s

25 r   25 r

3

From the back

4

From the front

5

Fold

Cut up to here

6

6. Stuff the legs and body with wool. Thread the hands through. The arms will be filled by the cotton-knit fabric but stuff them with a little more wool if they are too thin. Sew into place around the hands and the neck.

7. Sew small eyes using sewing thread. Count the stitches in the first eye and repeat for the second. Sew the mouth with pink thread. Sew the hair: you can choose any of the hairstyles from this book.

8. Tie a piece of wool around each ankle and make a bow. Sew a row of gathering stitches around the body under the arms to reduce the width slightly.

Ellie & Emma

This doll comes in two sizes: little Ellie, 24 cm (9 ½ in) and Emma, about 35 cm (13 ¾ in). The dolls Daniel and Daisy on pages 43 and 46 are sewn using the same pattern as Emma but in a different kind of cotton-knit fabric, which makes them a different size.

MATERIALS (THE LARGER MODEL)

- Flesh-coloured cotton-knit fabric: 28 x 35 cm (40 x 50 cm)/ 11 x 13 ¾ in (15 ¾ x 19 ¾ in)
- Tubular gauze: 15 cm, 3–4 cm wide (25 cm, 5 cm wide)/ 6 in, 1–1 ½ in wide (10 in, 2 in wide)
- Washed and carded sheep's wool: 50 g (150–200 g)/ 1 ¾ oz (5–7 oz)
- Strong two-ply wool warp yarn for the hair: 10 g (25 g)/ ⅓ oz (1 oz)
- Sewing thread in the same colour as the cotton-knit fabric and the hair, and pink thread for the mouth. For the eyes: thin buttonhole silk, wool or sewing thread
- About 2 cm (¼ in) rug warp or other strong thread
- Chopstick or plant stick to help with stuffing
- 7 cm (2 ¾ in) long darning needle with a big enough eye for strong thread such as rug warp
- Satin ribbon or thin plastic strips, about 1–2 cm (⅓–¾ in) wide
- If possible: felting needle and a sponge to rest on

1. Choose the size of doll, trace the pattern pieces on to paper and cut out (see page 38). Place the arms and head piece, which is placed along the fold, on folded cotton-knit fabric. Place the back side of the body and the front and back pieces of the legs on single fabric (figure 1). Draw round the pattern.

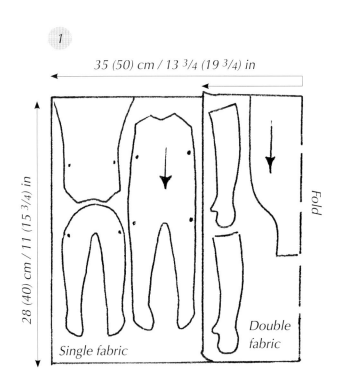

35 (50) cm / 13 ¾ (19 ¾) in

28 (40) cm / 11 (15 ¾) in

Fold

Single fabric

Double fabric

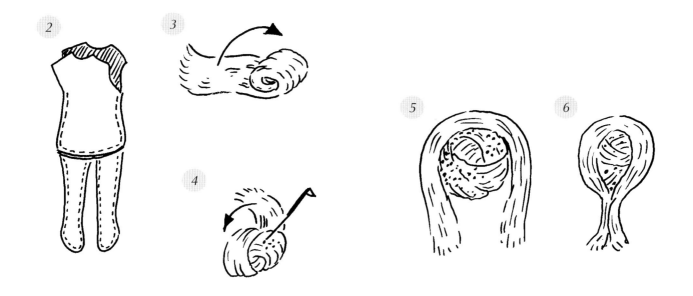

2. Sew with stretch stitch setting or very narrow zigzag, following the dotted lines of the pattern, 0.5 cm (¹/₄ in) inside the cut edge (= seam allowance). Pin together and sew the arms and head piece. Pin and sew legs up to the crotch. Pin and sew the body's back and front pieces along the sides, leaving an opening at the top. Finally pin and sew the rounded seam at the back (figure 2). Trim edges and turn all pieces the right way out.

3. For the head, prepare several long, wide but thin strips of sheep's wool or stuffing. Roll them tightly together to form a tight ball (figure 3). Change direction of the strips often (figure 4), at the same time pulling the strips tight to make a solid head ball. It will help if you use a felting needle from time to time to hold the wool in place.

4. When the ball is almost as big as the template on page 29, place a long wide strip of wool over it (figure 5) so that the ends reach underneath to form a neck (figure 6).

5. Lay a further strip of wool, crossing the first, going over the head and down to the neck

Ellie doesn't want her afternoon nap! She wants to play in her crib, even though Emma has made her bed so neatly. There's a party going on and they are both wearing their best white dresses (see pages 47 and 49). Sewing pillows for the cradle is simple: sew a bag about 16 x 20 cm (6 x 8 in). Turn the right way out. Fill with stuffing and sew the opening together. Decorate the pillow with bows or lace.

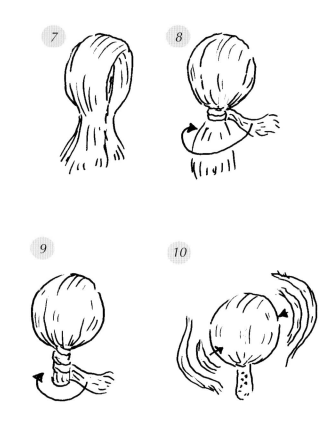

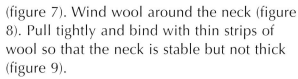

(figure 7). Wind wool around the neck (figure 8). Pull tightly and bind with thin strips of wool so that the neck is stable but not thick (figure 9).

6. If you have a felting needle you can add more wool to the chin and back of the head (figure 10), keeping it in place using the felting needle. The doll could also have a slight nose made from a small piece of wool, moulded with the felting needle.

7. When the head is the same size as the pattern (circumference about 18 cm/ 7 in for Ellie and 27 cm/ 10 ½ in for Emma) and has only slight resistance when squeezed, it's time for the gauze tubing. Tie the tubing at the top with strong thread and turn so that the knot is on the inside (figure 11). Pull the tubing over the head and tie with thread round the neck (figure 12).

8. Make marks on the sides where the ears are to be. Use strong thread and a darning needle at least 7 cm (2 ¾ in) long (if you do not have a long needle follow the instructions for Olga & Ollie for this step). Sew in from the centre back of the nape (leave a loose end) and through the head and out at one 'ear' (figure 13). Wrap the thread outside the head from

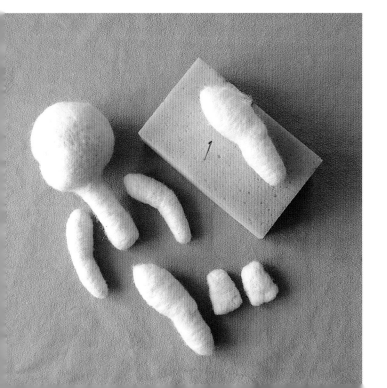

Here are the head, legs, feet and arms of the Emma doll. They are made first with tightly-wound wool and then shaped with the help of a felting needle. The felting needle is stuck into the sponge, which forms a very good base to protect you from the sharp point of the needle. Using the felting needle you can sculpt details such as the nose and knees. If you want a less sculpted doll, simply wind the wool pieces without using the felting needle. The doll's neck does not have to be as long as the one in the photo!

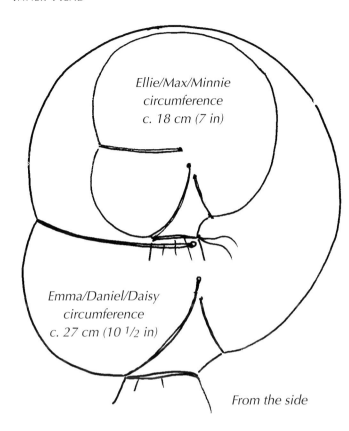

Ellie/Max/Minnie
circumference
c. 18 cm (7 in)

Emma/Daniel/Daisy
circumference
c. 27 cm (10 ¹/2 in)

From the side

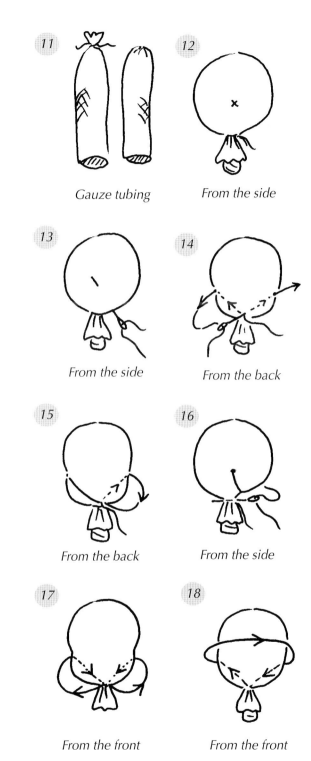

11

Gauze tubing

12

From the side

13

From the side

14

From the back

15

From the back

16

From the side

17

From the front

18

From the front

the ear round to the centre back, stick the needle back into the head at the nape and out at the other 'ear' (figure 14).

9. Pull so that the first thread outside the head is tight then wrap the thread as before, from the other ear back to the nape (figure 15). Stick the needle in at the centre back, right through the neck and out under the chin (figure 16). Pull tight again.

10. In the same way wrap the thread in two loops to mark the chin line: bring the thread from under the chin up to the ear, insert the needle back through to the throat, pull, then wrap a thread to the other ear, sticking the needle back down under the chin. Pull tight (figure 17).

11. Stick the needle in again and out at the ear, wrap a thread around the face at eye level to the other ear, insert the needle at the ear and out at the neck (figure 18) and pull so that the thread at eye level makes an indentation in the head. Tie the thread to the loose end at the neck. Tie a knot at the bottom of the tube so that it does not ride up when the head fabric is pulled on.

12. Pull on the head fabric from below with the seam at the back; the neck will come down into the narrow end. Stretch the fabric up over the head. Cut off any excess fabric, arrange the rest as if you were folding a parcel, turning in the loose ends and stitching in place by hand. Tie a thread under the chin (figure 19).

13. Stuff the arms, first putting a small wad of wool into each of the hands using the chopstick. Measure from the wrist up to the mark (figure 20). Leave the upper third of the arm empty.

14. Fold together a fairly thick strip of wool, the same length as the arm (figure 21).

15. Wind thin wool strips very tightly around the first strip (figure 22). Check that the arms do not become too long — if they do, fold down a piece of the upper arm and wind tightly. Bend the arm slightly while you wrap the wool round (figure 23).

16. Wind on more wool as evenly as possible and thicker at the top. If you have a felting needle you can lay the wool in different

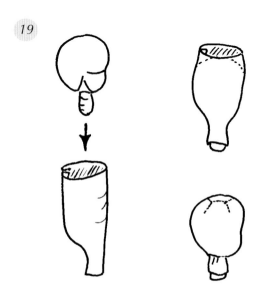

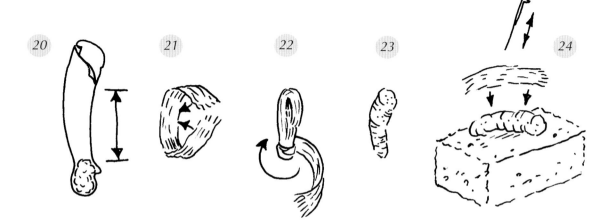

directions and fasten in place with the felting needle (figure 24).

17. Do the other arm, making sure it is the same size as the first. Insert the arms into the arm fabric, just as you would pull on a sock. If it's difficult to get the wool arm into the fabric you can place a ribbon or strip of plastic cut along the arm, round the lower end and up again (figure 25). When the arm is completely inserted down to the wrist, pull out the ribbon or strip of plastic (figure 26).

18. Place the arms together, thumbs pointing outwards (figure 27) and sew across the upper ends, joining the arms.

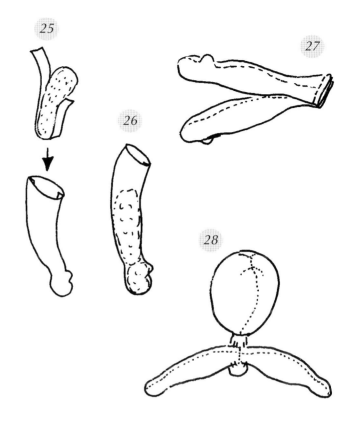

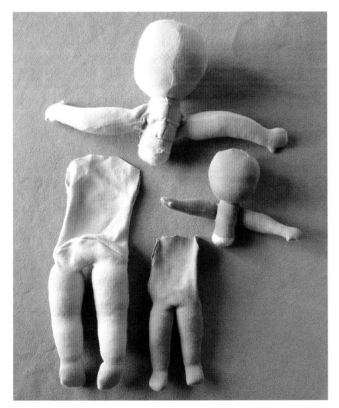

The same pattern in two different sizes makes the dolls Emma and Ellie. Here you can see how the parts are sewn together. Emma's body and head are lying face downwards. Ellie's body parts face upwards.

19. Position the arms 1 cm (1/3 in) down the back side of the neck with the thumbs pointing forwards and sew them in place with a few stitches (figure 28).

20. The legs are stuffed in the same way as the arms, but are filled all the way up to the groin. Fold wool together into two small 'parcels' to form the feet, and stuff them right down into the legs. Measure from the ankle as far as just below the groin and use that length when you fold a thick strip of wool to be the leg, which is then wrapped tightly in wool. The thighs should be a lot thicker than the lower leg. Wind on thin strips of wool, one at a time. The legs can be moulded using a felting needle. Insert the wool legs into the fabric, using a plastic strip or ribbon as for the arms.

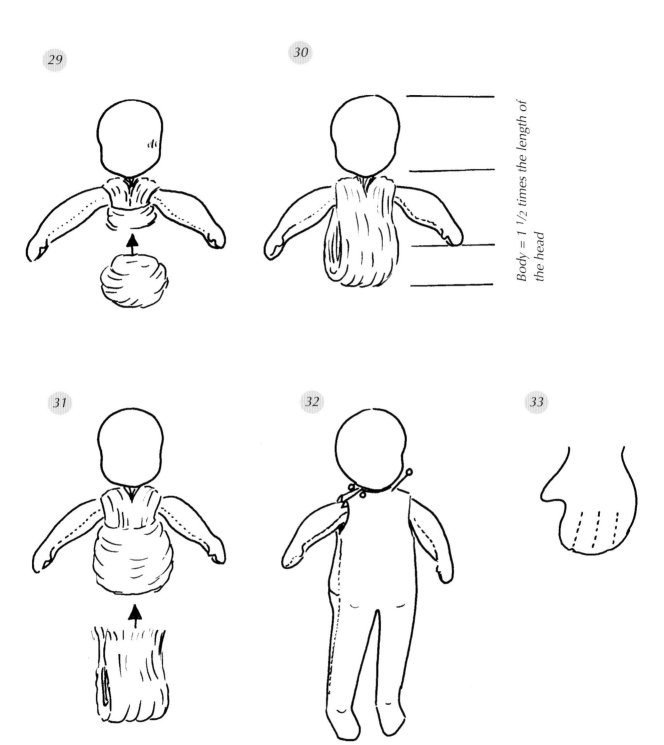

29

30

Body = 1 ½ times the length of the head

31

32

33

21. Wrap wool around the doll's neck and shoulders. Then roll a round ball of wool for the stomach, almost as big as the head (figure 29).

22. Lay a thick layer of wool, as wide as the body, around the stomach ball and up around the doll's front and back. Divide the wool at the throat and continue down the other side of the body (figure 30). The body should be about 1 $\frac{1}{2}$ times the length of the head.

23. Wind a thin layer of wool horizontally across the doll's stomach and then a further vertical layer (figure 31). Now it's time to put the whole thing into the body fabric. Fold in the seam allowance at the top of the back and stomach side of the fabric and place four pins in at the throat (figure 32).

24. Sew the body fabric tightly to the neck using catch stitch (see page 11), just above the thread that is tied round it. If necessary push in more wool under the arms or in the stomach. Turn in the seam allowance and sew the length of the shoulder seams using small, close stitches. If the side seams do not reach all the way up to the armpits, sew them together until they do. Finally, fold in the seam allowance of the body fabric and attach it at an angle round the arms. If the doll is to have fingers, sew three seams in the hand, starting with the middle seam (figure 33).

25. Use thin wool yarn or buttonhole silk for the eyes and sewing thread for the mouth. Sew the eyes as small half-suns or triangles. Count the stitches used in the first eye and sew the same number in the second. The mouth is sewn once the eyes are in place, either with a couple of horizontal stitches or as a row of tiny slanting stitches. The eyes and mouth are placed so that they form an equilateral triangle.

26. Use thin wool yarn for the hair, such as two-ply, strong warp yarn. Stitch in place with sewing thread the same colour as the hair yarn, or with the hair yarn itself.

Ellie's hair

Draw the hairline with a faint pencil line. Embroider long stitches like sunrays (A, p.34) making shorter stitches into the head, and longer ones on top (B). When the whole head has been covered with yarn, sew long, free-hanging loops spread over the head (C) with fixed stitches in between (D). Cut the loops. It's easiest to start from the outside and work towards the middle.

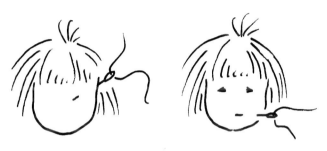

Push in needle from the side

Eye Stitches

Daniel and Daisy   *Ellie and Emma*

Mouth Stitches

Ellie and Daisy   *Emma and Daniel*

Ellie

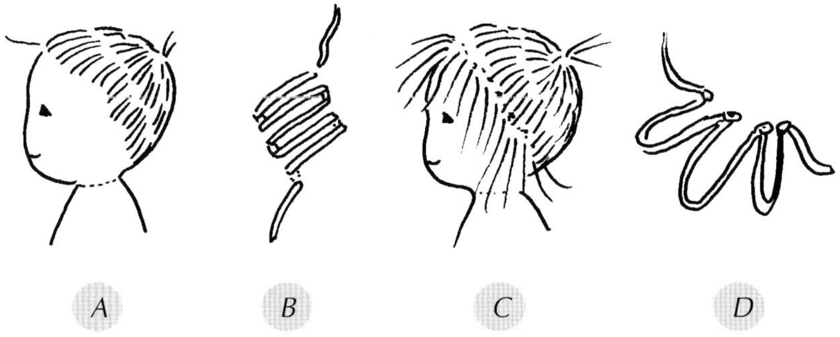

A   B   C   D

Daisy

A   B   C

Daniel

A   B   C

Emma

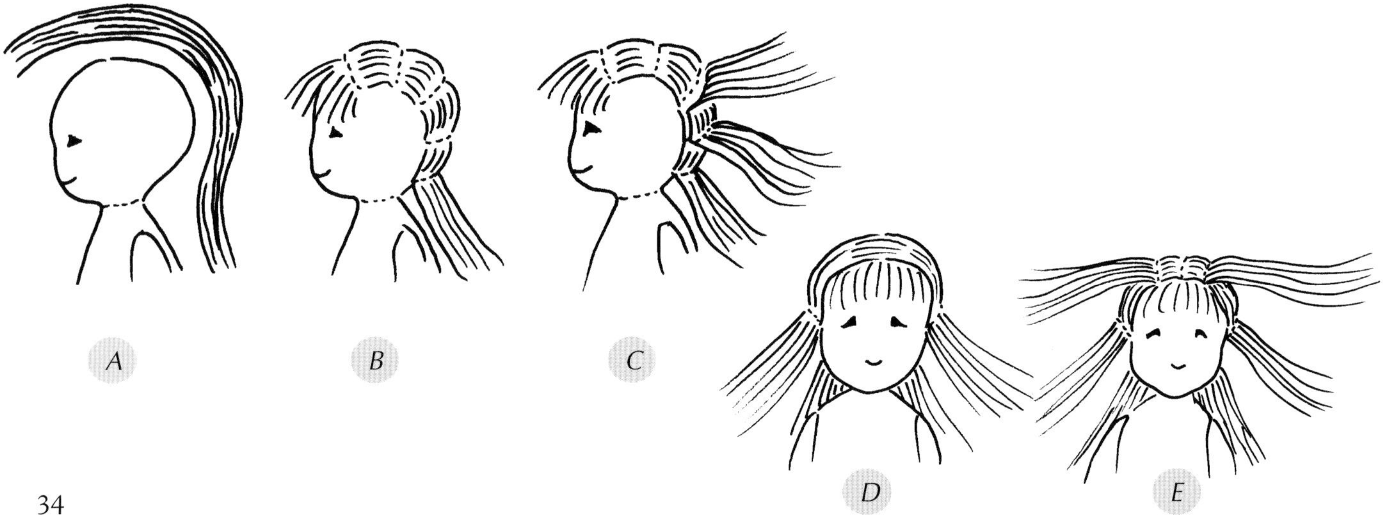

A   B   C   D   E

34

Daisy's hair

Lay lengths of yarn across the head (A). Sew the hair in place with a centre parting and with two seams above the ears which meet at the back (B). Spread the hair towards the back of the neck (C). Lift the top layer of hair at the back and sew the underneath layer so that the neck is covered.

Daniel's hair

Knit or crochet a square using the yarn you plan to use for the hair. Wet the square and let it dry properly. Then undo the work, and you will have curly yarn. Arrange lengths of curly yarn as a covering base layer of hair (A). Using sewing thread, sew several seams horizontally across the head (B). Ruffle up the remaining hair into a tangle and attach to the head with stitches here and there, leaving long loose loops as untidy locks (C).

Emma's hair

Cut a thin layer of lengths of hair, as long as you prefer, to run from the fringe and down the back (A). Spread it out evenly and attach with horizontal seams (B). Measure a thin layer of hair that reaches from the back to above the nape and down again. Sew it into place with two horizontal seams about 2 cm (3/4 in) apart, above the neck seam (C). Now place a layer of hair from side to side, at right angles across the previously attached hair. Sew it into place above the ears (D). Lay a last layer over the first, sewing it in place with a centre parting and then two seams parallel to the middle parting but above the ear seams (E). Even the hair with scissors and have fun making your own hairstyle!

Ellie is always happy when she can run about out of doors. Her hair is sewn as an embroidered base layer with longer threads left loose above it. Instructions for her dress are on page 39.

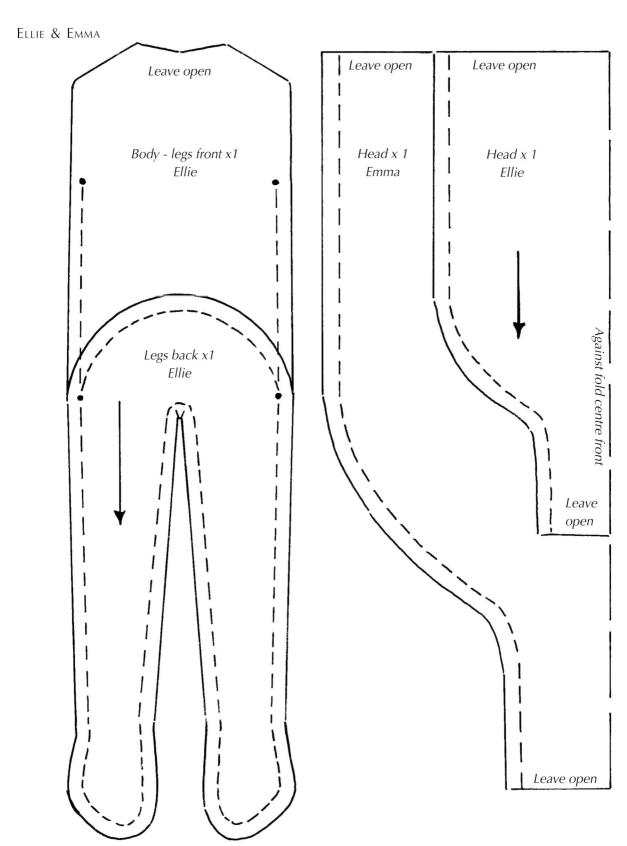

Leave open

Body - legs front x1
Ellie

Legs back x1
Ellie

Leave open

Leave open

Head x 1
Emma

Head x 1
Ellie

Against fold centre front

Leave open

Leave open

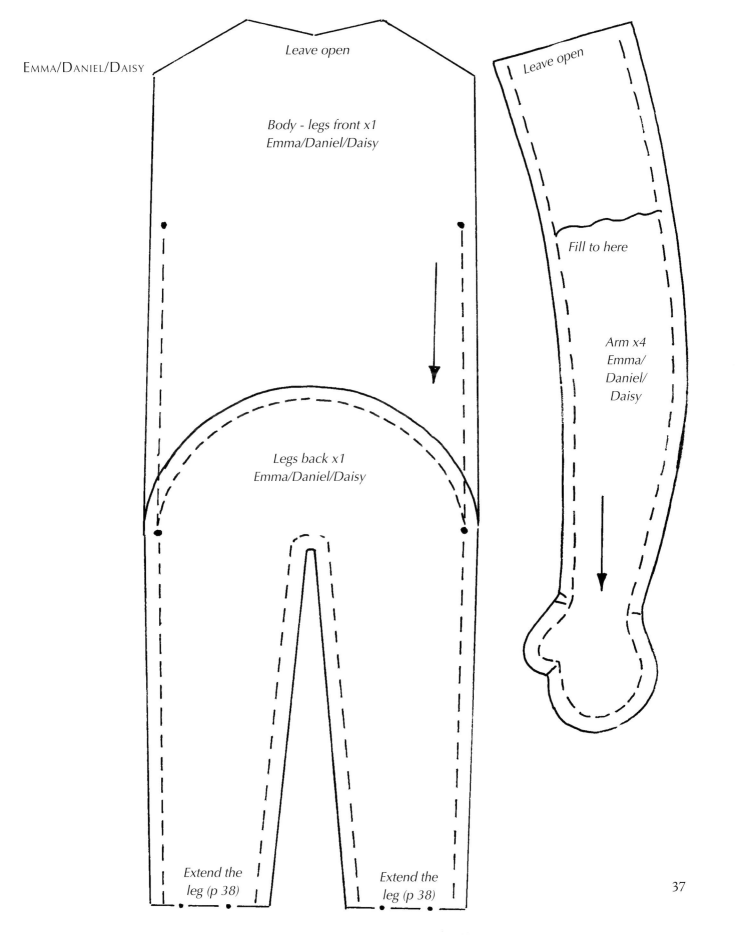

EMMA/DANIEL/DAISY

Leave open

Body - legs front x1
Emma/Daniel/Daisy

Legs back x1
Emma/Daniel/Daisy

Extend the
leg (p 38)

Extend the
leg (p 38)

Leave open

Fill to here

Arm x4
Emma/
Daniel/
Daisy

37

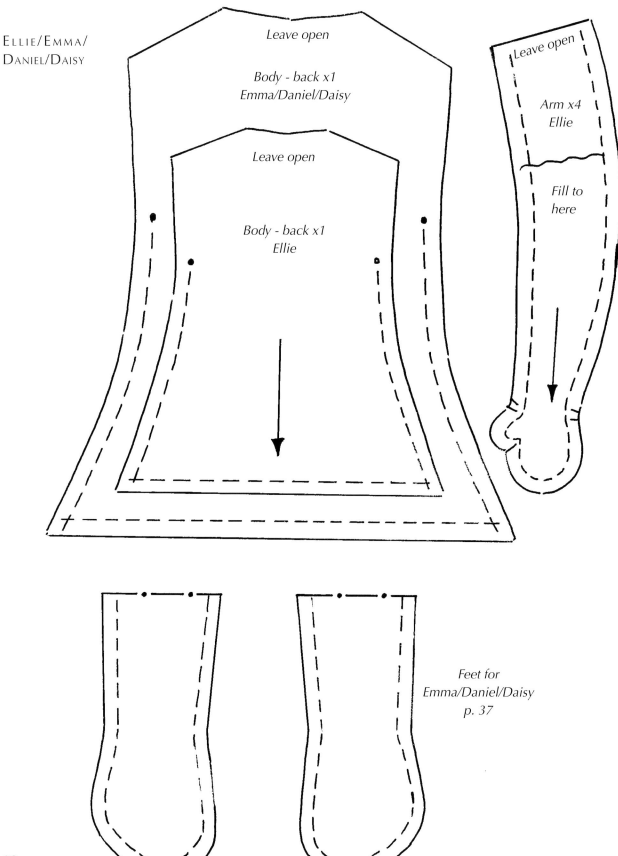

Ellie/Emma/
Daniel/Daisy

Leave open

Body - back x1
Emma/Daniel/Daisy

Leave open

Body - back x1
Ellie

Leave open

Arm x4
Ellie

Fill to
here

Feet for
Emma/Daniel/Daisy
p. 37

38

Clothes for Ellie, Emma, Daniel and Daisy

Ellie's Dress

1. Cut out the pieces in thin felt following the pattern on page 47.
2. Sew the shoulder seams.
3. Attach the sleeves to the bodice.
4. Sew arm and side seams in one.
5. Gather the skirt so that it fits the bodice and sew them together.
6. Turn in and sew the edges at the back.
7. Attach a ribbon to tie at the back in a bow.
8. Sew a decorative trim around the hem, if desired.

Wide trousers

1. Cut out the pieces in thin jersey or cotton material following the pattern on page 48. Zigzag around the edges of the pieces.
2. Turn up and sew the hem at the bottom of the leg, thread elastic through, pull tight and secure with a few stitches on each side.
3. Sew the leg seams.
4. Sew the centre front and back seams in one.
5. Turn in and sew a hem at the waist and thread elastic through.

Shirt

1. Cut out pattern pieces in cotton material following the pattern on page 49. Zigzag around all edges. Turn in and sew seam allowance at the back and around the neck, or make an edging (with 40 cm/ 16 in bias binding).
2. Turn up and sew hems at the cuffs. Thread elastic through Emma's shirt, pull tight and stitch in place.
3. Sew arm and side seams. Leave open for a split at the bottom of Daniel's shirt.
4. Turn in and hem around the splits each side of Daniel's shirt. Hem the bottom. Sew a lace edging on Emma's shirt.
5. Sew ribbon, press fasteners or a button and buttonhole at the back.

Hat

1. Cut out the pieces from felt following the pattern on page 50.
2. Sew together the hat crown's six triangles, three and three together first.
3. Sew together both brims along the outer edge.
4. Attach the crown to the brim.

Lined cap

1. Cut out the pieces in the same fabric as the trousers, following the pattern on page 50.
2. Sew together the six triangular pieces for the lining and the outer layer individually. Put the hat lining inside, wrong sides facing.
3. Put an edging around the crown of the cap, sewing the lining and outer layer together at the same time.
4. Sew together the lining and outer layer of the peak, turn the right way out and sew to the cap's inside.

Trousers with straps

1. Cut out the pieces in cotton material following the pattern on page 51.
2. Turn up the hem at the bottom of the trousers and sew.
3. Sew the leg seams.
4. Sew the centre back and centre front seam.
5. Pin two pleats at the front and two at the back, in the middle. Try the trousers on the doll before you sew the waistband in place.
6. Turn in the seam allowance on the straps and fold them double, right side out. Sew along the long side and one short side.
7. Sew on the straps at the back and try for length.
8. Stitch buttonholes and sew on buttons on the waistband at the front.

Woolly jumper

1. Cast on stitches using size 2 or 2.5 needles (mm)/ 14 or 13 (UK) 0 or 1 (US). Knit a tension sample for a few rows to get 16 cm (6 $1/3$ in) width. See the pattern on page 52.
2. Knit in garter stitch for 7 cm (2 $3/4$ in).
3. Increase 9 cm (3 $1/2$ in) each side for the arms.
4. Knit 6 cm (2 $1/3$ in).
5. Cast off 11 cm (4 $1/3$ in) in the middle for the neck and cast on the same number of stitches at the same place on the next row. Measure to ensure the neck goes over the doll's head.

6. Knit 6 cm (2 $1/3$ in).
7. Cast off along the arms, 9 cm (3 $1/2$ in) each side.
8. Knit 7 cm (2 $3/4$ in). Cast off.
9. Sew together arm and side seams.
10. If you like, crochet a row of stitches round the neck opening.

Sandals

1. Cut out pieces in leather following the pattern on page 52.
2. Glue the ends of the straps to the sole.
3. Glue the inner sole in place.

Brown bag

1. Cut out pieces in leather following the pattern on page 52.
2. Sew a button towards the top of the front piece.
3. Glue the front piece to the lower part of the back piece with a thin line of glue along the edges.
4. Sew a seam around the glued edges.
5. Cut a buttonhole on the folded-over part of the back piece.
6. Glue on a shoulder strap.

Emma is so warm in the sunshine! She has made herself look pretty with a ribbon in her hair to have tea with Daniel. He is wearing his trousers with straps, a smart white shirt (see page 39) and sandals. On the grass is his matching cap. The little teddy is described on page 56.

Vest

1. Cut out the pieces from thin cotton jersey following the pattern on page 53.
2. Sew the shoulder seams.
3. Sew the side seams.
4. Turn under and sew with zigzag round the armholes, neck and lower edge.

Panties

1. Cut out the pieces from thin cotton jersey following the pattern on page 53.
2. Turn under and zigzag the hems on the legs.
3. Sew the leg seams.
4. Sew the crotch seam.
5. Turn under and sew the waist.

Dress

1. Cut out pieces from felt following the pattern on page 54.
2. Sew the shoulder seams.
3. Turn under and sew the cuffs.
4. Sew the arms to the bodice.
5. Sew arm and side seams in one.
6. Gather and sew the skirt waist to the bodice.
7. Hem the skirt at the bottom.
8. Turn under and sew the neck and the back edges.
9. Sew on press fasteners at the back.

Knitted hat

1. Cast on stitches in red wool and knit a tension sample in stocking stitch to be 22 cm (8 2/3 in) wide. See the pattern on page 55.
2. Knit 2 cm (3/4 in). The whole hat is knitted in stocking stitch.
3. Knit the contrasting pattern in black wool. Knit 2 stitches in red and then *1 black, 3 red*, repeating from * to * for as many rows as you have room for, finishing with 2 red. Turn and knit an identical row back. Then knit 2 rows with 3 black, 1 red. End with 1 black row.
4. Knit 3 cm (1 in) in red.
5. Cast off 7 cm (2 3/4 in) at both ends.
6. Continue knitting in red until the centre part measures 7 cm (2 3/4 in). Cast off.
7. Sew the back together, A to A and B to B (see pattern page 55).
8. Pick up about 25 stitches from the lower edge, knit rib (1 plain, 1 purl) for 3 rows. Cast off.
9. Make a braid and thread it through the ribbed edge.
10. Sew white lace inside the front edge.

Ellie is fidgeting in the pram and Daniel is making sure she is comfortable. Daisy is wearing her warm red dress and a knitted hat (see above). Daniel is wearing a woolly jumper (see page 41). The doll's pram is designed by Kerstin Rehnman.

White bag

1. Cut out the parts in leather following the pattern on page 55.
2. Glue the front part to the back part along the edges.
3. Glue the flap to the top of the back piece.
4. Sew a seam around the glued edges.
5. Sew on a button at the front and cut a buttonhole in the flap.
6. Glue on the shoulder strap.

Shoes

1. Cut out the pieces from felt following the pattern below.
2. Sew together the upper part of the shoe.
3. Sew on the sole all round.
4. Sew on a button and make a loop from wool.

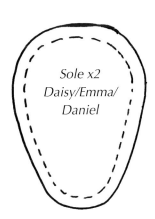

*Sole x2
Daisy/Emma/
Daniel*

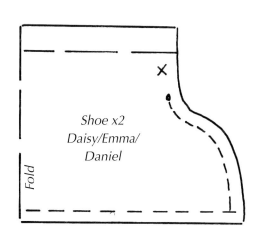

*Shoe x2
Daisy/Emma/
Daniel*

Fold

Emma has done the washing and now she's hanging up the clothes on the line to dry in the wind. It's so warm she is wearing only her vest (see page 42).

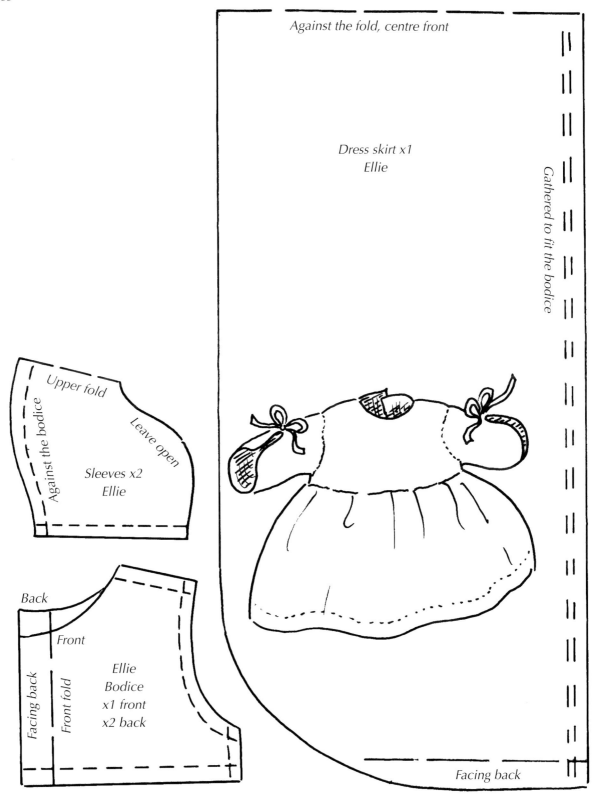

Against the fold, centre front

Dress skirt x1
Ellie

Gathered to fit the bodice

Upper fold

Leave open

Against the bodice

Sleeves x2
Ellie

Back

Front

Facing back

Front fold

Ellie
Bodice
x1 front
x2 back

Facing back

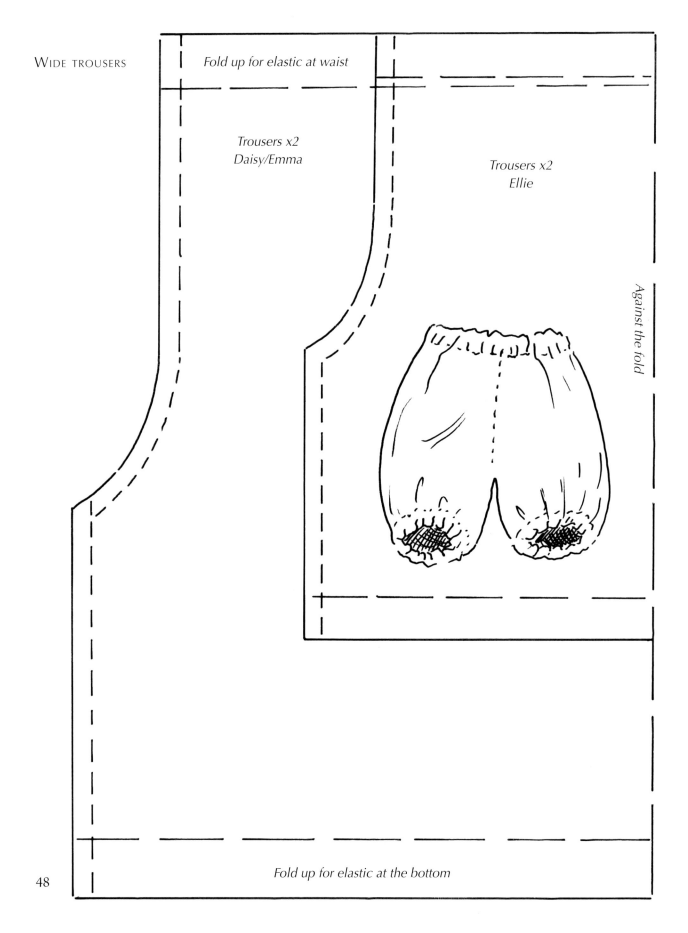

Fold up for elastic at waist

Trousers x2
Daisy/Emma

Trousers x2
Ellie

Against the fold

Fold up for elastic at the bottom

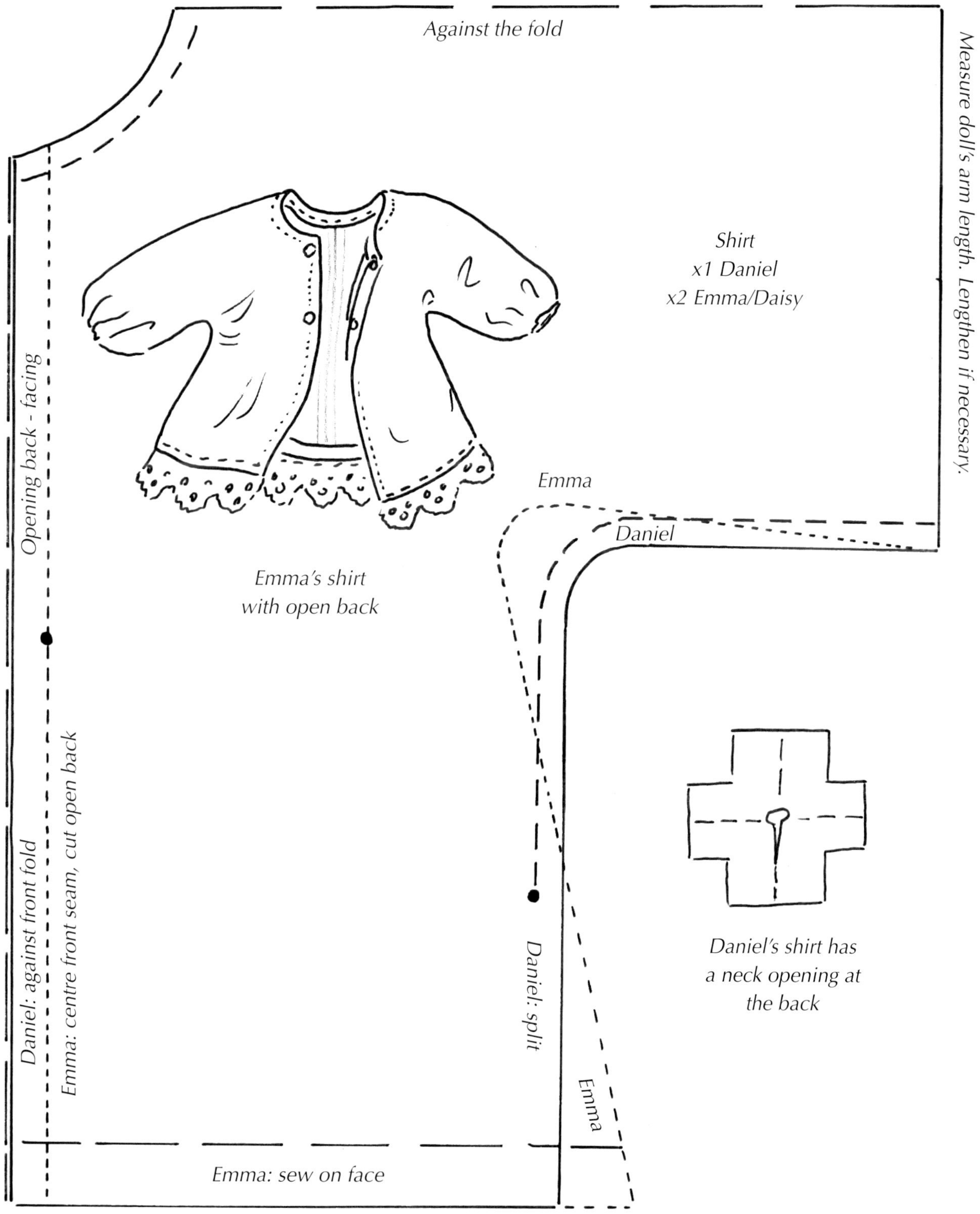

SHIRT

Against the fold

Measure doll's arm length. Lengthen if necessary.

Opening back - facing

Shirt
x1 Daniel
x2 Emma/Daisy

Emma

Daniel

Emma's shirt
with open back

Daniel: against front fold

Emma: centre front seam, cut open back

Daniel: split

Emma

Daniel's shirt has
a neck opening at
the back

Emma: sew on face

49

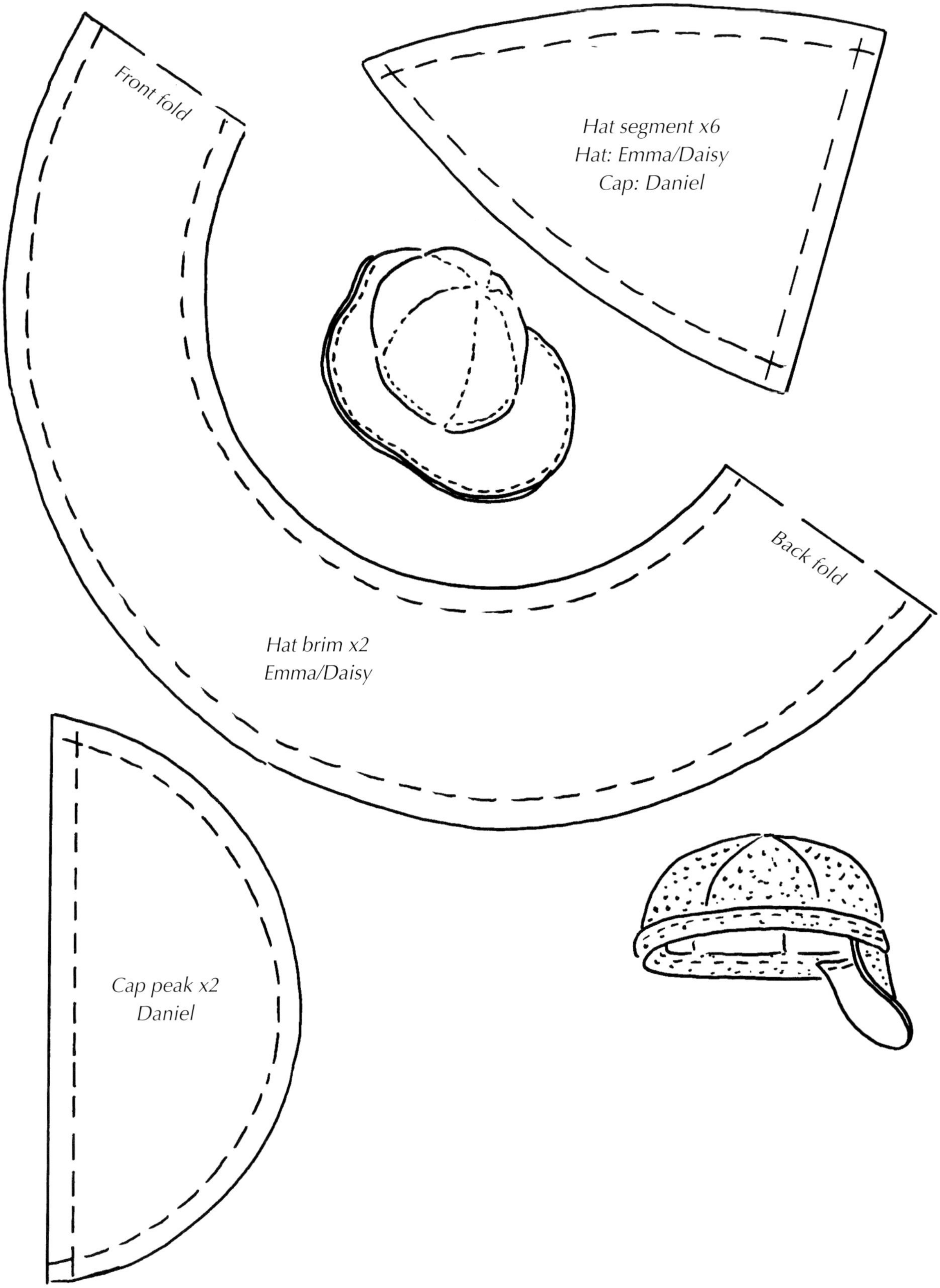

Front fold

Hat segment x6
Hat: Emma/Daisy
Cap: Daniel

Back fold

Hat brim x2
Emma/Daisy

Cap peak x2
Daniel

1 waistband: 5 x 35 cm (2 x 13 ³/4 in)
2 straps, each: 5 x 22 cm (2 x 8 ²/3 in)

Make a pleat - try on the doll

Trousers x2
Daniel/Emma/Daisy

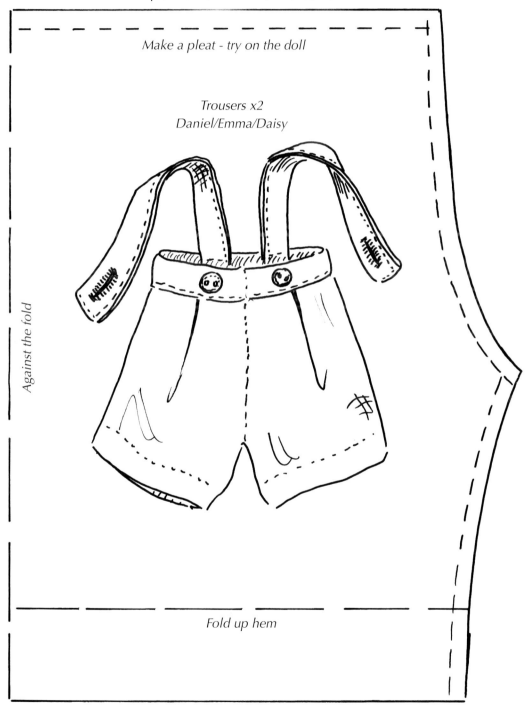

Against the fold

Fold up hem

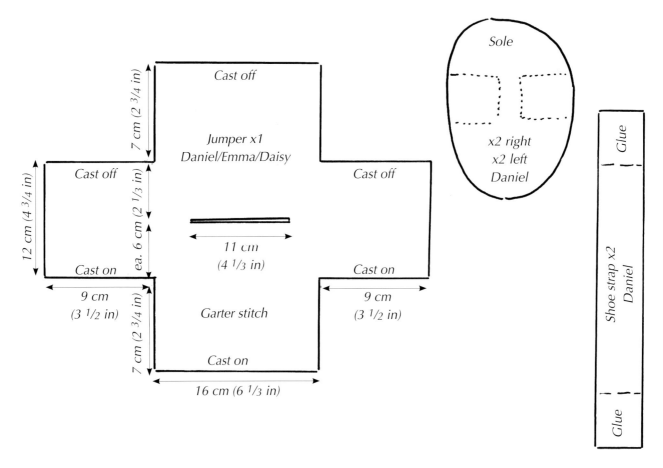

Sole

x2 right
x2 left
Daniel

Glue

Shoe strap x2
Daniel

Glue

7 cm (2 ³/4 in)

Cast off

Jumper x1
Daniel/Emma/Daisy

Cast off

ea. 6 cm (2 ¹/3 in)

Cast off

12 cm (4 ³/4 in)

Cast on

Cast on

11 cm
(4 ¹/3 in)

9 cm
(3 ¹/2 in)

9 cm
(3 ¹/2 in)

7 cm (2 ³/4 in)

Garter stitch

Cast on

16 cm (6 ¹/3 in)

Shoulder strap 1 x 35 cm (13 ³/4 in)

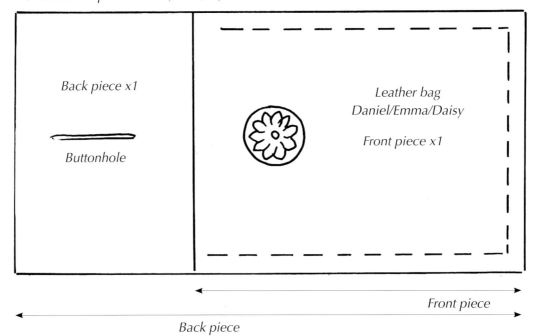

Back piece x1

Buttonhole

Leather bag
Daniel/Emma/Daisy

Front piece x1

Front piece

Back piece

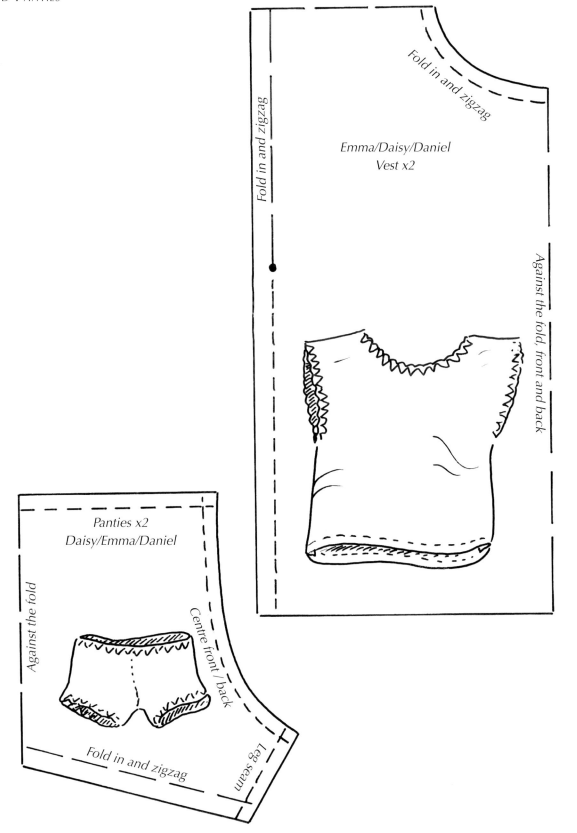

Fold in and zigzag

Fold in and zigzag

Emma/Daisy/Daniel
Vest x2

Against the fold, front and back

Panties x2
Daisy/Emma/Daniel

Against the fold

Centre front / back

Leg seam

Fold in and zigzag

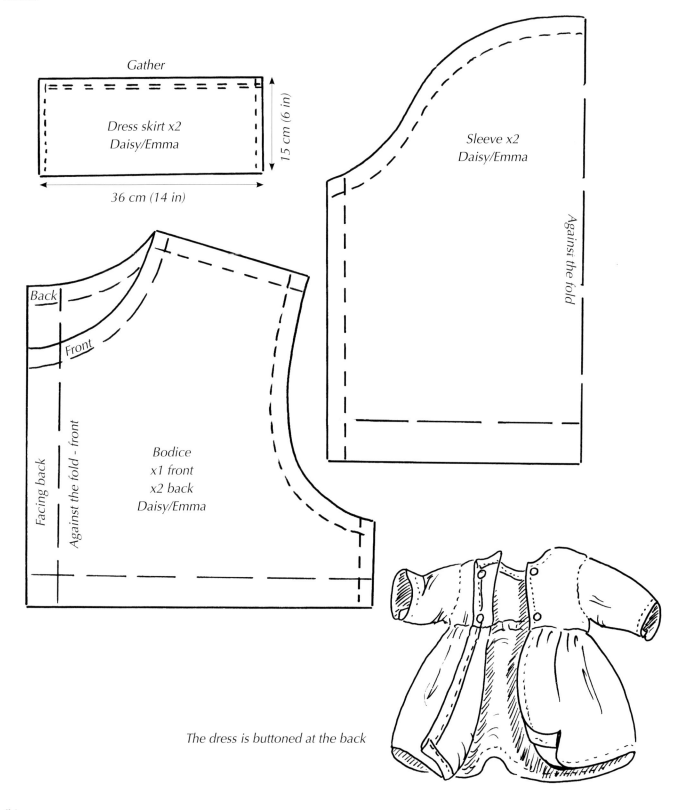

Gather

Dress skirt x2
Daisy/Emma

15 cm (6 in)

36 cm (14 in)

Sleeve x2
Daisy/Emma

Against the fold

Back

Front

Facing back

Against the fold - front

Bodice
x1 front
x2 back
Daisy/Emma

The dress is buttoned at the back

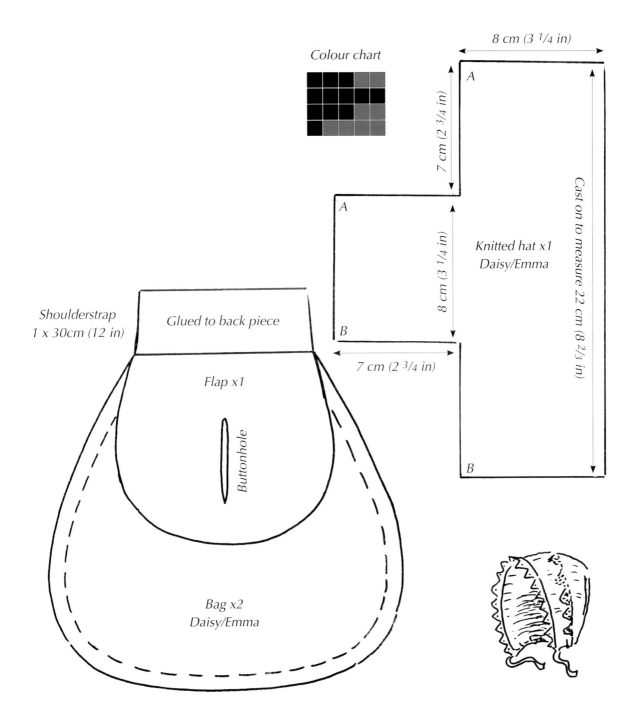

Colour chart

8 cm (3 1/4 in)

A

7 cm (2 3/4 in)

A

8 cm (3 1/4 in)

B

7 cm (2 3/4 in)

Knitted hat x1
Daisy/Emma

Cast on to measure 22 cm (8 2/3 in)

B

Shoulderstrap
1 x 30cm (12 in)

Glued to back piece

Flap x1

Buttonhole

Bag x2
Daisy/Emma

Teddy

Make a little teddy for one of the dolls, sewn in real teddy fabric and with movable limbs. This one is 13 cm (5 in) long. See the photographs on pages 40 and 46.

MATERIALS
- 18 x 20 cm (7 x 8 in) teddy fabric or other sturdy fur fabric
- 20 g (3/4 oz) stuffing wool
- Dark brown thread for the nose and eyes
- Strong thread and a long darning needle

1. Trace the pattern on to the wrong side of the fabric. Cut out the pieces.
2. Pin, tack and sew together the seams around the four legs. Sew the body, first the centre front from A to B, and then both side seams from C to D. Lastly fold down the nose flap and stitch it from C to A on both sides. Cut the small nicks in the seam allowance as shown on the pattern.

3. Turn the right way out.
4. Stuff all the parts as hard as you can. Sew up the openings.
5. Sew on the arms and legs in the same way as for Max and Minnie (see page 90).
6. Embroider eyes and nose.

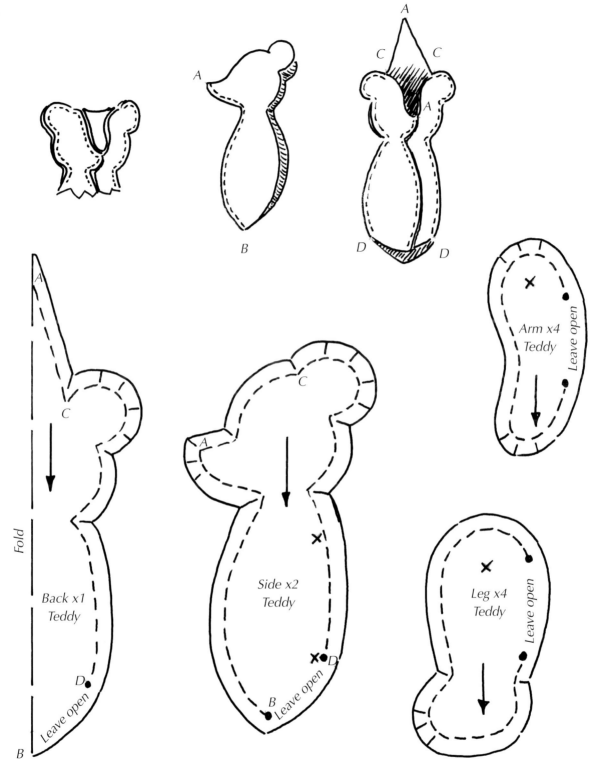

Olga & Ollie

These large baby dolls are 48 cm (19 in) tall. Ollie's body is shorter because more fabric was folded in under the chin. Hair and clothes can give the dolls different characters. The clothes patterns follow directly after the doll instructions.

MATERIALS

- Flesh-coloured cotton knit, folded double: 50 x 70 cm (19 2/3 x 27 1/2 in)
- Washed and carded stuffing wool: 300 g (10 1/2 oz)
- Gauze tubing: 5 cm (2 in) wide, 30 cm (12 in) long
- Embroidery thread or buttonhole silk for the eyes
- Sewing thread for the mouth and hair
- Strong, two-ply wool warp yarn (or angora wool) for the hair: 25–50 g (1–1 3/4 oz)
- Rug warp or other strong cotton thread
- Chopstick or plant stick to stuff with
- 30 cm (12 in) long, 2 cm (3/4 in) wide strip of thin plastic or equivalent satin ribbon
- If you have it: felting needle and sponge to rest on
- A sheet of tissue paper (for Ollie's hair)

1. Trace the pieces on to paper and cut them out. Place them on a piece of folded flesh-coloured cotton knit with the arrow in the direction of the ribbing. Place the head piece along the fold (figure 1). Draw round the pieces on to the material. Sew all seams along the dotted line with the stretch setting.

2. Cut out the body. Sew the three darts at the bottom of the front and back pieces. Sew the pieces right sides together along the sides and the groin. Sew the other pieces. Trim the seam allowance to 1/2 cm (1/4 in). Flatten the seams at the toes and sew a curved seam across the bottom of each foot (figure 2).

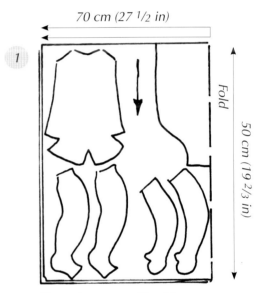

Place the pattern like this on double fabric

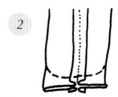

It's fun to play in the hay! But now Ollie wants to take Olga for a ride in the cart. They have kicked off their shoes, described on page 74, where you will also find Olga's jumper and leggings. Instructions for Ollie's dungarees are on page 73.

3. Turn all pieces right side out except the body. Rub the fabric together on the right side to work out the thumbs.

4. Prepare several long, wide and thin strips of wool. Wind them into a hard ball, making sure they do not twist (see the instructions for Ellie and Emma on page 27). Pull the strips, stretching and winding them as tightly as you can, so that the ball is firm (fasten in place from time to time using a felting needle). When the ball is almost as big as the template on page 61 take two wide, 50 cm (19 $^2/_3$ in) long strips of stuffing wool and place them in a cross over the head, (figure 3). Pull the strips down under the head and wind wool round to form a neck/backbone. Fasten with the felting needle. Wind more wool around the neck/backbone. Make the neck stable. If you have a felting needle you can add more wool to the chin and back of the head, and secure it using the felting needle.

Make the cheeks wide. The circumference of the head should be about 35 cm (13 $^3/_4$ in).

5. Knot the gauze tubing at one end, turn inside out and thread this bag over the doll's head. Tie a length of rug warp under the chin.

6. Cut 1.5 m (5 ft) of rug warp. Wrap the thread twice around the middle of the head (figure 4). Position the knot at one ear. Wind one end under both strands to tie, so that the knot stays done up when you pull (double over-hand knot). Pull so that the thread makes an indentation in the ball. Make another knot, (figure 5).

7. Take the thread and pass it over the top of the head to the other ear, tie it to the thread encircling the head so that it is stretched over the crown. Sew a cross with sewing thread at each ear so that the knots stay in place (figure 6).

8. Bring down the neck thread to about 1 cm ($^1/_3$ in) above the throat thread, (figure 7). Wind the loose threads hanging down at the

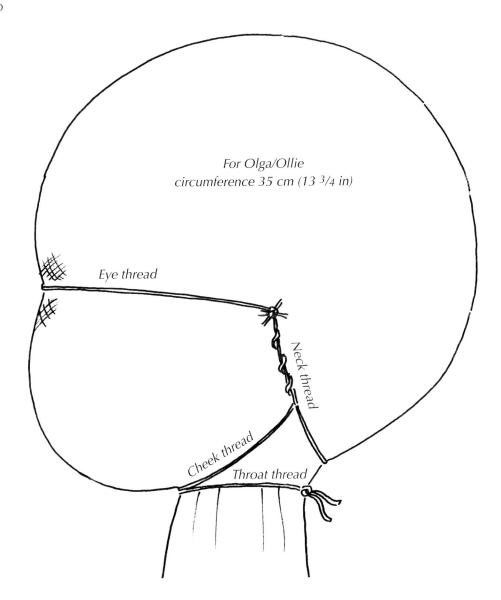

For Olga/Ollie
circumference 35 cm (13 3/4 in)

Eye thread

Neck thread

Cheek thread

Throat thread

Inner head definition

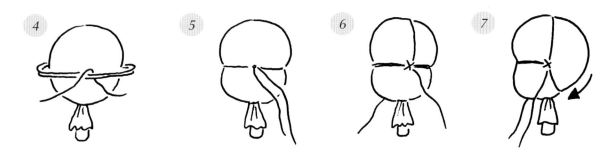

ears around the neck three times and let them cross at the front under the chin (figure 8), then tie them at the back (figure 9). The shaping of the head is now finished (figure 10). If you end up with a lumpy shape resembling mumps, you can sew backwards and forwards through the neck under the ears and pull tight.

9. Place the inner head, neck first, into the cotton knit bag. Make sure the seam is at the centre back (figure 11).

10. Stretch the fabric up over the crown. Attach the fabric first around the lower part of the neck and then sew the top (figures 12 & 13). If there is not enough fabric, cut out a round piece to cover the top of the head. If there is too much fabric, trim some away. When you have finished sewing the top of the head tie a

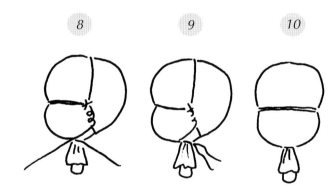

From the front

The inner head for Ollie and Olga. The head is first made by winding carded wool into a ball. Using a felting needle helps the wool to stay in place. When the ball is sturdy and a good shape, gauze tubing is threaded over it and strong thread (rug warp) tied round it following the instructions, to shape the eyeline and nape of the neck.

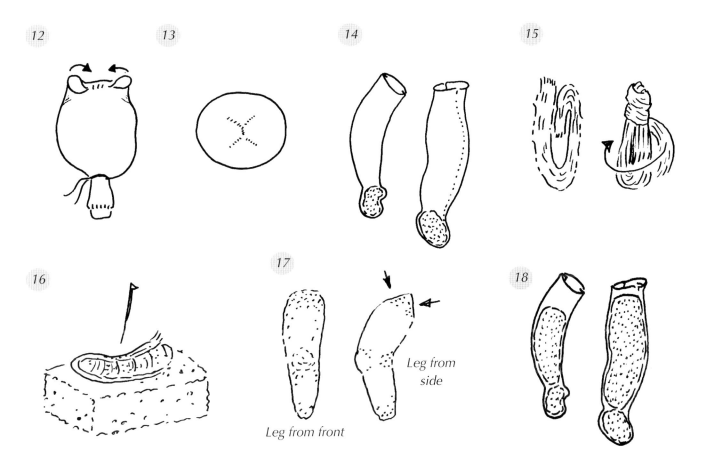

Leg from front

Leg from side

strong thread around the neck, with the knot at the back. It's important that the fabric is stretched so that there are no wrinkles under the chin.

11. Using a stuffing stick, fill the hands and feet (figure 14). If you want narrow, neat feet you can shape two rectangular feet with the help of a felting needle (resting on a sponge underlay to protect yourself and the needle) and then push them in.

12. Stuff the arms and legs. Measure the length of the arm from the wrist to the mark. Leave the upper third of the arm empty. Leg length: measure from the ankle and almost all the way up, leaving a couple of centimetres as a seam allowance. Fold thick strands of wool lengthwise for the leg lengths (figure 15).

13. Wind the measured strands of wool tightly with wide, thin strips of wool (figure 15). Pull, wind, stretch and secure, preferably using a felting needle, (figure 16). Wind on more wool, a little at a time. Make the limbs thicker at the top.

14. Let the arms bend forward slightly, and the legs backwards behind the knees. Using a felting needle the legs can be made a little flatter at the back and front towards the top (figure 17). Check that the arms and legs match.

15. Insert the wool arms and legs into the cotton-knit fabric (figure 18). If it's difficult to

insert them, lay a strip of plastic or a satin ribbon, about 2 cm (3/4 in) wide, along the length of the arm or leg, round the end and back up again, and that will make it easier (see the photograph below). When the wool is properly inserted, right down into the hands and feet, pull out the ribbon or plastic. Pull the fabric up over the filling.

16. Lay the legs side by side, with the toes pointing outwards a little. Thread the body piece over them, wrong side out, until the toes stick out from the neck opening at the base of the body fabric. Adjust the fabric and tack the legs in place right through the fabric of the body and the legs, as in figure 19 and the photograph below.

17. Turn up the body fabric and make sure the legs are nicely in place. Fold the fabric back again and sew the seam securely. Turn the fabric up again (figure 20).

18. Sew the upper ends of both arms together, thumbs pointing outwards. Sew across using the machine (figure 21). With a few stitches, secure the arms behind the neck, a few centimetres from the throat thread, with the thumbs pointing forwards.

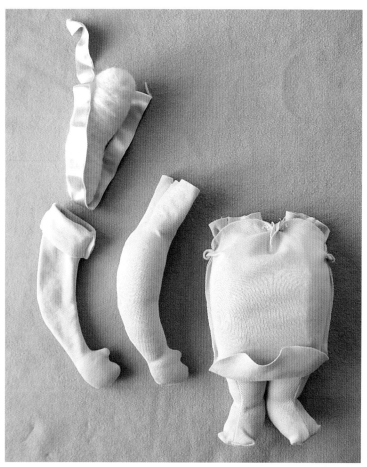

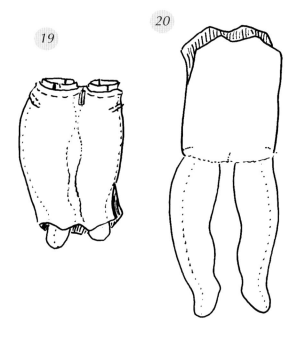

The body piece for Olga and Ollie is pulled on over the stuffed, completed legs, wrong side out, and sewn so that the legs are attached. After that the body fabric is folded upwards. If it's difficult to insert the tightly-wound legs and arms, use a satin ribbon or strip of plastic to help.

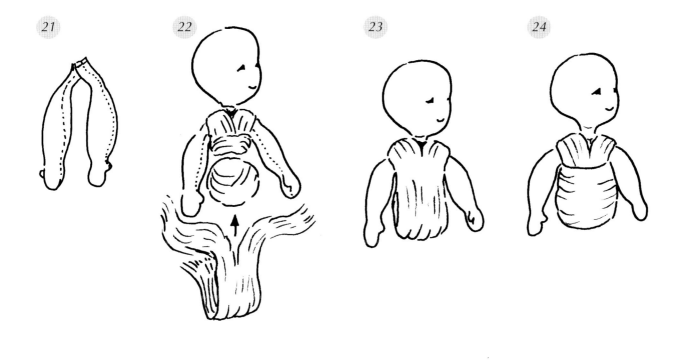

19. Wrap wool around the backbone and over the shoulders. Roll a ball for the stomach, shaping with the felting needle, to put under the backbone. The stomach can be as thick as the head (figure 22).

20. Bind the stomach ball in place at the head and arms with wide strips of wool which divide at the shoulders, pass down over the back and come up over the stomach again (figures 22 & 23).

21. Wrap a thin layer of wool horizontally round the stomach and all the way up to the armpits (figure 24). Then place another layer of wool vertically over the stomach and back.

22. When the body seems sufficiently full insert it into the body fabric. Turn in the seam allowance at the upper edges of the stomach and back, holding the fabric in place with pins at the neck. Using small, neat stitches sew the body fabric securely at the neck and sew the shoulders together. Use backstitch or catch stitch (see page 11). Before sewing round the arms, push a little more wool into the shoulders or armpits if necessary. The doll should feel really crammed full of wool!

23. Sew eyes using thin, shiny embroidery thread or buttonhole silk. Sew many horizontal stitches first, slightly fan-shaped, and then some vertical stitches to hold the longer, flatter stitches together, giving the doll a more awake appearance (see page 33).

24. Embroider the mouth using pink thread.

Olga's hair

Using a pencil, draw a faint line around the doll's head immediately above the place where the hairline is to be (A). Begin with a thin covering layer of wool from the fringe back over the head. Sew it in place with seams going across the head. Carry the layer down to where the ears are to be (B). Add in a layer, double the required length, which will cover the back of the head from ear to ear. Sew it in place with two seams, an upper and a lower, a couple of centimetres above the hair-line at the nape of the neck (B & C) and fold the top piece over. Lay another layer of hair over the head from side to side, above the fringe (C) and sew in place with a centre parting and a further seam on each side (D). Finally place a thick layer of fringe and hair that goes back over the crown (E). Sew it in place above the fringe and in the middle of the head. Divide it into two layers and sew the under layer further down the back of the head (F). Even out the hair and style it (G).

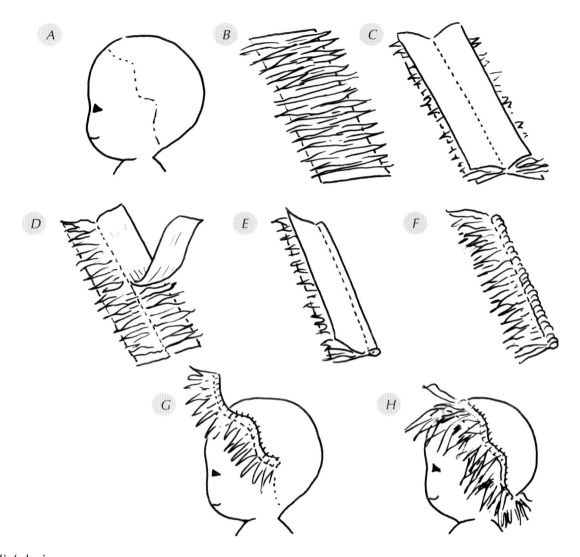

Ollie's hair

Using a pencil, draw a faint line around the doll's head immediately above the place where the hairline is to be (A). Cut long strips, about 10 cm (4 in) wide, of tissue paper. Take parallel lengths of wool or yarn and place them across the paper, evenly distributed (B). When one strip of paper is full, place another piece the same size over the top and, if necessary, pin them together in one or two places along the sides. Using the machine sew with straight stitch and the smallest stitch length down the middle of the paper, with the hair in between (C). Tear away the upper paper (D) and fold the hair and lower sheet of paper in two (hair on the inside). Sew another seam 1 cm (1/3 in) from the folded edge (E). Tear away the remaining paper. You now have a fringe (F). Continue making fringes as you sew on the hair, so that you do not make too many.

Attach the fringes using sewing thread the same colour as the hair. Sew a seam in the fringe's folded edge (G), sewing about 1 cm (1/3 in) of the fringe flat on to the head. Begin sewing around the hairline and work in a spiral towards the crown of the head (H). Trim the hair to even it out.

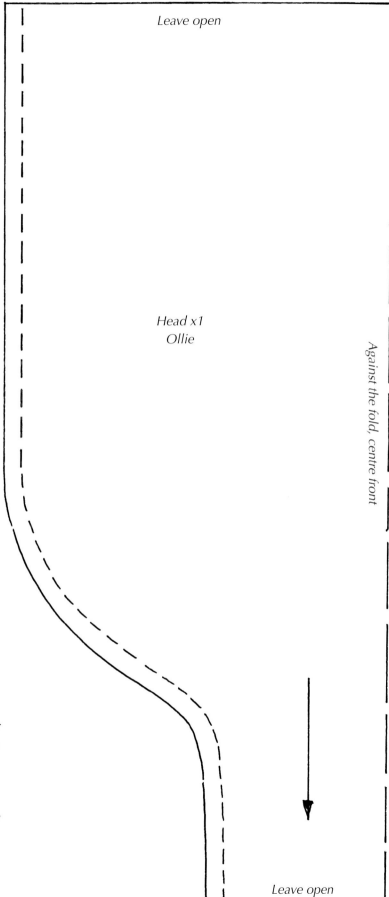

Leave open

Head x1
Ollie

Against the fold, centre front

Leave open

Olga is very impatient, waiting for Ollie to finish using the potty. She wants to carry on playing! Ollie's hair is made from angora wool and Olga's from strong, two-ply wool warp. Olga's trousers can be found on page 82.

69

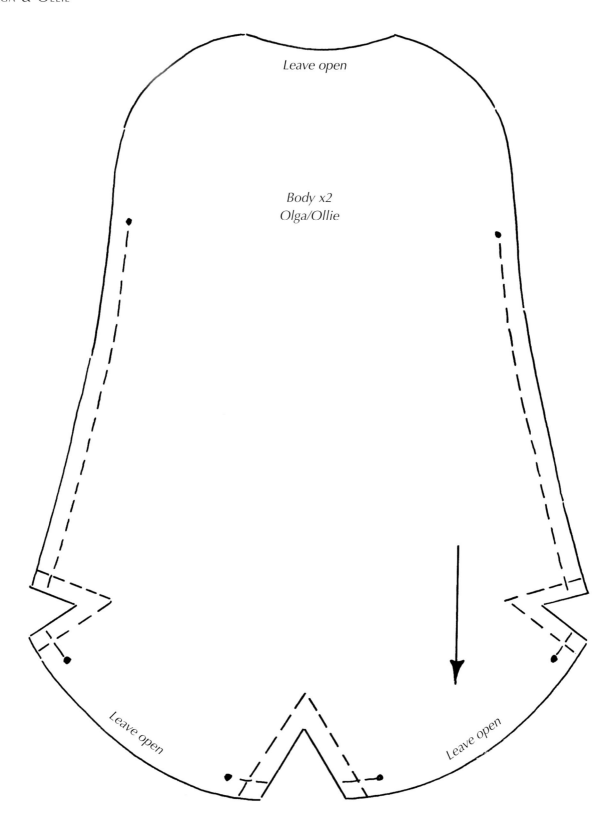

Leave open

Body x2
Olga/Ollie

Leave open

Leave open

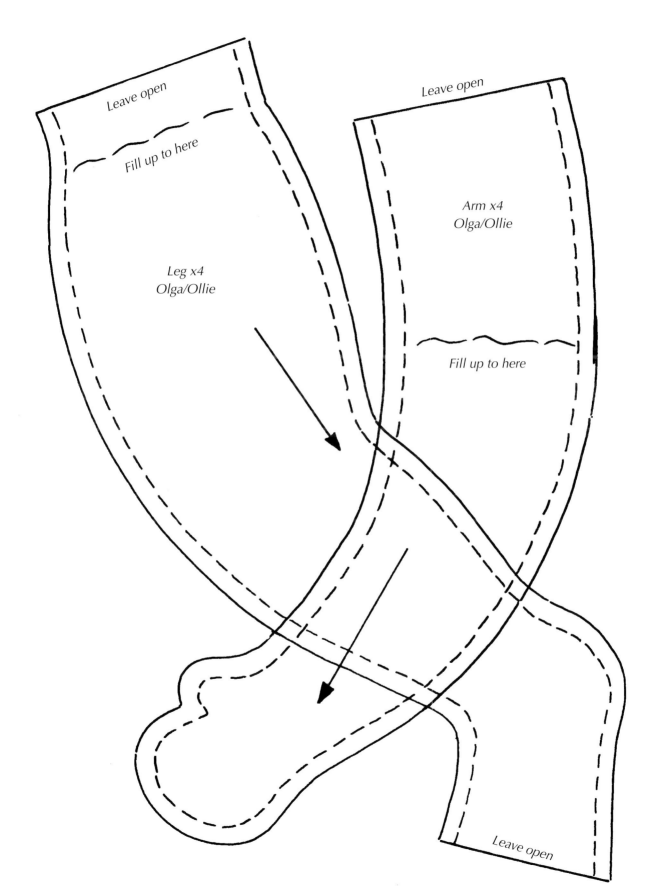

Leave open

Fill up to here

Leg x4
Olga/Ollie

Leave open

Arm x4
Olga/Ollie

Fill up to here

Leave open

71

Ollie and Olga's clothes

Dress

1. Cut out pieces in thin cotton material following the pattern on page 78.
2. Sew together the shoulder seams.
3. Sew a band around the neck.
4. Sew the sleeves to the bodice.
5. Turn up the cuffs and sew a double seam wide enough for the elastic a short way up the sleeve. Thread the elastic through, pull the fabric tight and fasten the elastic on each side in the seam allowance.
6. Sew the sleeve and side seam as one seam.
7. Fold in and stitch facings in the bodice back.
8. Fold in and stitch the edges of the back slit in the skirt.
9. Sew together the two skirt side seams.
10. Gather the waistband of the skirt so that it fits the bodice and attach with straight stitch, right sides facing.
11. Turn up the hem, sewing with straight stitch.
12. Sew press fasteners at the back.

Dungarees

1. Cut out the pieces following the pattern on page 79.
2. Hem the legs. Olga: turn up and sew a seam at the bottom of each leg. Ollie: turn up and sew two seams, 1 cm ($1/3$ in) apart. Both: thread elastic through, gather the fabric and secure the elastic on each side.
3. Sew the leg seams.
4. Sew the centre back and front seams as one.

5. Olga: turn in and sew a double seam at the top for the elastic. Finished!
6. Ollie: gather the width at the waist, measure against the doll. Sew together the waistband's short ends. Fold the waistband in two, lengthwise, right side out, sew it to the trousers, right sides facing, and turn it up.
7. Fold the front flap double, right sides facing, sew together one long side and both short sides. Turn.
8. Sew the front flap to the waist at the centre front.
9. Turn in the seam allowance of the straps and fold them double, right sides out. Sew along the long side and one short side, attach the straps to the waistband at the back. Try on the doll.
10. Sew buttonholes at the end of each strap and fasten two bright buttons on to the front flap.

Boots

1. Cut out the pieces from soft leather following the pattern on page 80.
2. Sew together along the centre front, right sides facing.
3. Cut small nicks in the seam allowance at the base. You can put in an extra insole at this stage.
4. Make holes for the laces and thread leather strips through.

What a present! Olga steps out of the box and on to the birthday table on a sunny summer's day. Instructions for her dress and boots are above, and her long johns are on the next page.

Fur fabric socks

1. Cut out pieces in fur fabric following the pattern on page 80.
2. Fold the sock double with the pile inwards and sew according to the markings. Turn.
3. Sew four small balls by pulling tight the gathering stitches around the circle and pushing in a little stuffing.
4. Stitch the balls to thin ribbon and tie a ribbon around each sock.

Shirt

1. Cut out the shirt pieces from white cotton fabric following the pattern on page 81. Note! The sleeves must be lengthened by 9 cm (3 1/2 in).
2. Turn in the cuffs and sew a double seam for the elastic a short way up the arm.
3. Sew a lace edging at the bottom of the arm.
4. Thread elastic through, gather the sleeve and fasten the elastic on each side.
5. Sew the sleeve and side seams in one.
6. Hem the bottom of the shirt.
7. Zigzag stitch round the neck and the back edges. Turn under and sew down the seam allowance.
8. Sew on ribbons to tie at the back, or use press fasteners.

Long johns

1. Cut out the pieces in stretchy cotton jersey following the pattern on page 82.
2. Fold the trouser cuffs double, wrong sides facing. Place the cuffs against the lower edge of the legs, right sides facing, stretch them slightly, pin and sew in place.
3. Sew the leg seams.
4. Sew the centre back and front seams in one.
5. Sew together the short ends of the waistband. Fold the waistband double along its length, wrong sides facing, and place it right sides facing along the upper edge of the trousers. Stretch the waistband a little, pin and sew in place.
6. Thread elastic through if needed.

Woollen jumper

1. Knit a tension sample cuff in rib (1 plain, 1 purl) so that the knitting is 21 cm (8 1/4 in) wide. See the pattern on page 83.
2. Knit rib for 10 rows then change to stocking stitch. Knit until the work measures 16 cm (6 1/3 in).
3. Cast off 13 stitches for the neck in the middle of the next row. Cast on 13 stitches in the same place on the next row.
4. Carry on until the back is as long as the front, finishing with 10 rows of rib. Cast off.
5. Pick up stitches for the sleeve in the middle of the long side, 16 cm (6 1/3 in), and knit about 10 cm (4 in) in stocking stitch, knit 6 rows of rib for the cuff and then cast off. The sleeve should be about 12 cm (4 3/4 in) long. Knit the other sleeve in the same way.
6. Sew the arm and side seams.
7. Thread a crocheted drawstring around the neck.

Hat

1. Knit a tension sample so that the work measures 35 cm (13 3/4 in) in width. Knit 3 cm (1 in) rib. See the pattern on page 83.
2. Knit stocking stitch for 10 cm (4 in).
3. Knit a row of holes (knit 2 together, take wool over needle, for the whole row)
4. Knit 3 cm (1 in) rib then cast off.
5. Crochet a drawstring and make two tassels from wool. Thread the string through the holes, pull and tie.
6. Attach the tassels to the ends.

Mittens

1. Knit a tension sample in rib so that the work measures 6 cm (approx 2 in) in width. Knit 3 cm (1 in) rib. See the pattern on page 83.
2. Knit stocking stitch for 6 cm (2 in).
3. Knit 2 stitches together for the rest of the row. Thread yarn through the stitches, pull together and fasten. Sew the mittens' longs sides together.
4. Crochet a string 40 cm (15 3/4 in) long and sew one end to the cuff of each mitten.
5. If the mittens are too wide at the cuff, thread a braid through and tie a bow.

Jacket

1. Cut out the jacket in cotton material, the cuffs and one collar in jersey, and one collar in fur fabric, following the pattern on page 84.
2. Sew the shoulder seams together.
3. Fold the cuffs of the sleeves double, wrong sides facing, stretch them slightly, pin and then stitch to the bottom of the sleeves.
4. Sew the side and sleeve seams in one.
5. Turn in the front edges and sew in a zip.
6. Sew together the short ends of the waistband. Fold it double lengthwise, wrong sides facing.

Ollie is dressed for a bracing ride in the snow. Hat instructions are on page 74, mittens and jacket are above.

Place it against the lower edge of the jacket, right sides facing, stretch, pin and sew in place.

7. Collar: Lay the jersey fabric on top of the fur fabric, right sides facing, sew the short ends and one long side. Turn the right way out. Sew the open side to the neck of the jacket, right sides facing, fur fabric facing out. Push the seam allowance into the neck and sew using straight stitch from the right side.

Nappy

1. Cut out two pieces of cotton jersey fabric following the pattern on page 85.
2. Sew all around except for one short side. Turn and stuff with wool.
3. Sew the opening. Sew a long tape to each short side.

Bib

1. Cut out the two bib pieces in cotton fabric or vinyl-coated fabric, as on page 85.
2. Sew them together around the outer edge, right sides facing, turn and press.
3. Fold in and sew the neck edge.
4. Push tape into the open ends and sew in place.
5. Sew a lace edging all round.

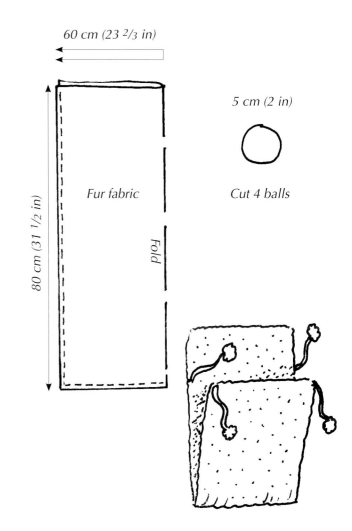

60 cm (23 2/3 in)

5 cm (2 in)

Fur fabric

Cut 4 balls

80 cm (31 1/2 in)

Fold

How typical! You have to change a nappy while you're out walking with the pram. Sew the cosy sleeping bag in fur fabric: cut a piece 60 x 80 cm (23 2/3 x 31 1/2 in), fold double lengthwise, right sides facing. Sew along both long sides and one short side, turn right side out and sew up the opening. Make four small balls (see description for fur fabric socks, page 74). Attach the balls to strings and attach the strings as in the diagram above.

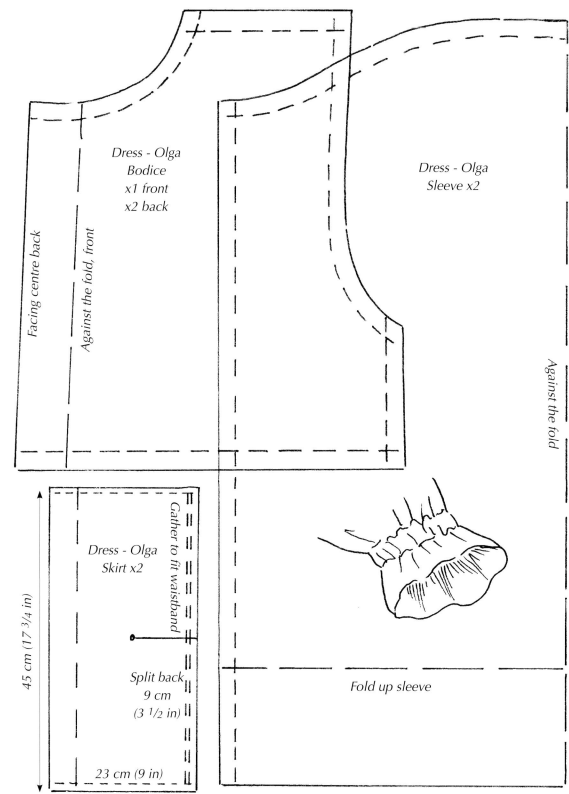

Dress - Olga
Bodice
x1 front
x2 back

Dress - Olga
Sleeve x2

Facing centre back

Against the fold, front

Against the fold

Dress - Olga
Skirt x2

Gather to fit waistband

45 cm (17 ³/4 in)

Split back
9 cm
(3 ¹/2 in)

23 cm (9 in)

Fold up sleeve

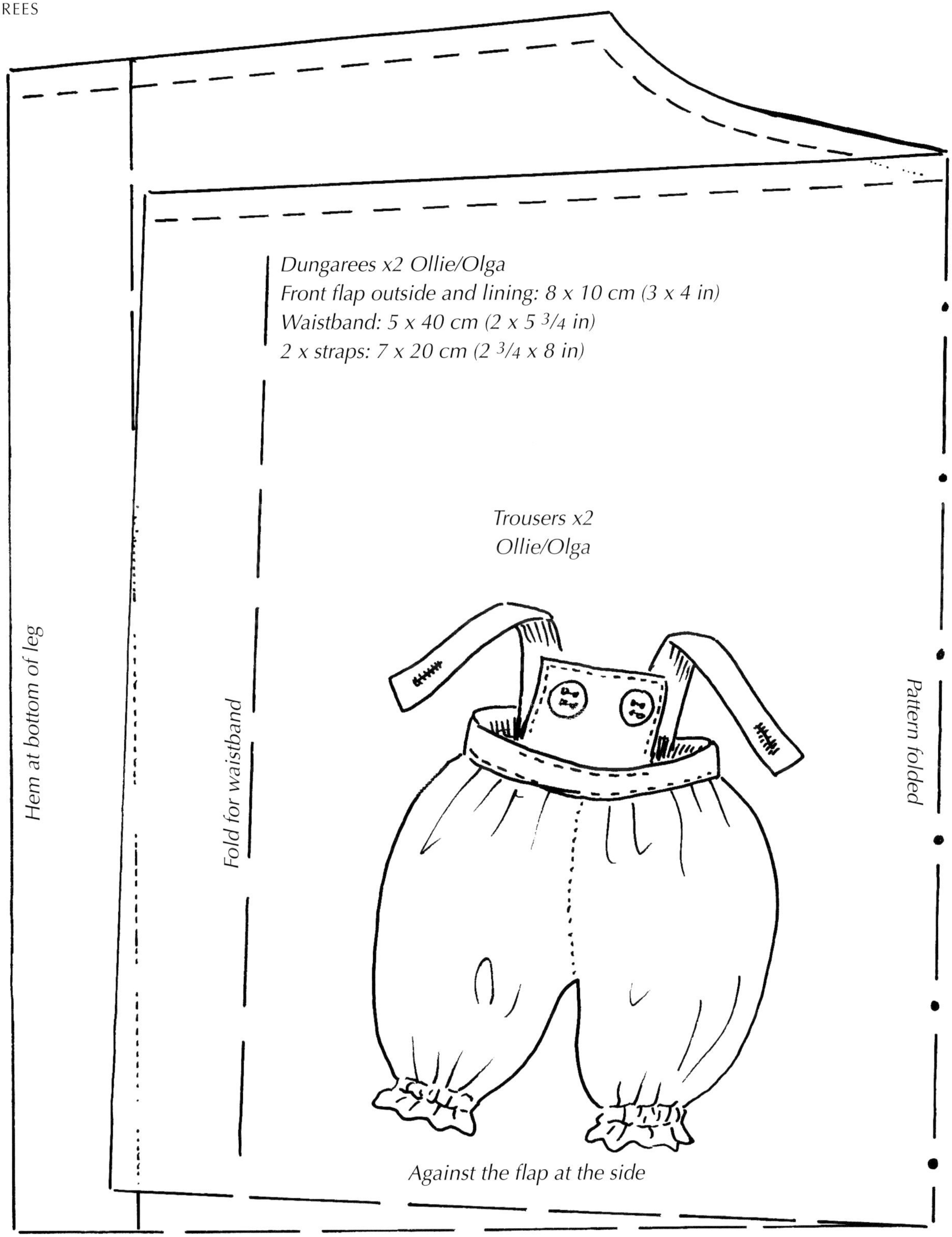

Dungarees x2 Ollie/Olga
Front flap outside and lining: 8 x 10 cm (3 x 4 in)
Waistband: 5 x 40 cm (2 x 5 ¾ in)
2 x straps: 7 x 20 cm (2 ¾ x 8 in)

Trousers x2
Ollie/Olga

Hem at bottom of leg

Fold for waistband

Pattern folded

Against the flap at the side

79

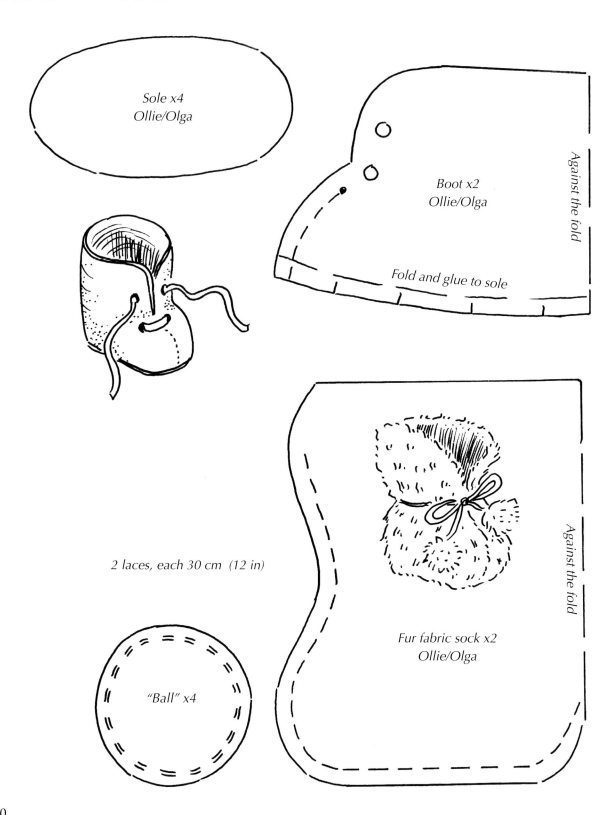

Sole x4
Ollie/Olga

Boot x2
Ollie/Olga

Against the fold

Fold and glue to sole

2 laces, each 30 cm (12 in)

Against the fold

Fur fabric sock x2
Ollie/Olga

"Ball" x4

Against the fold

Shirt x1
Ollie/Olga

Extend sleeve straight, 9 cm (3 ½ in)

Against the fold, front. Edge back.

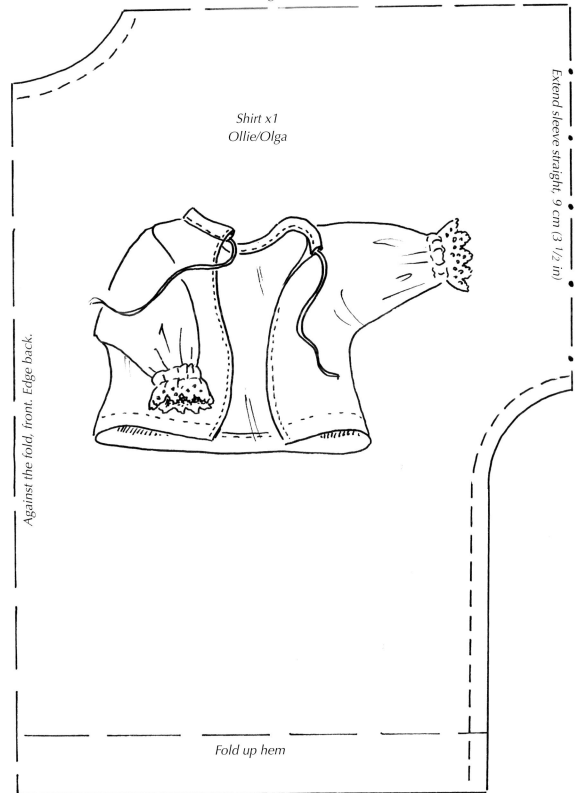

Fold up hem

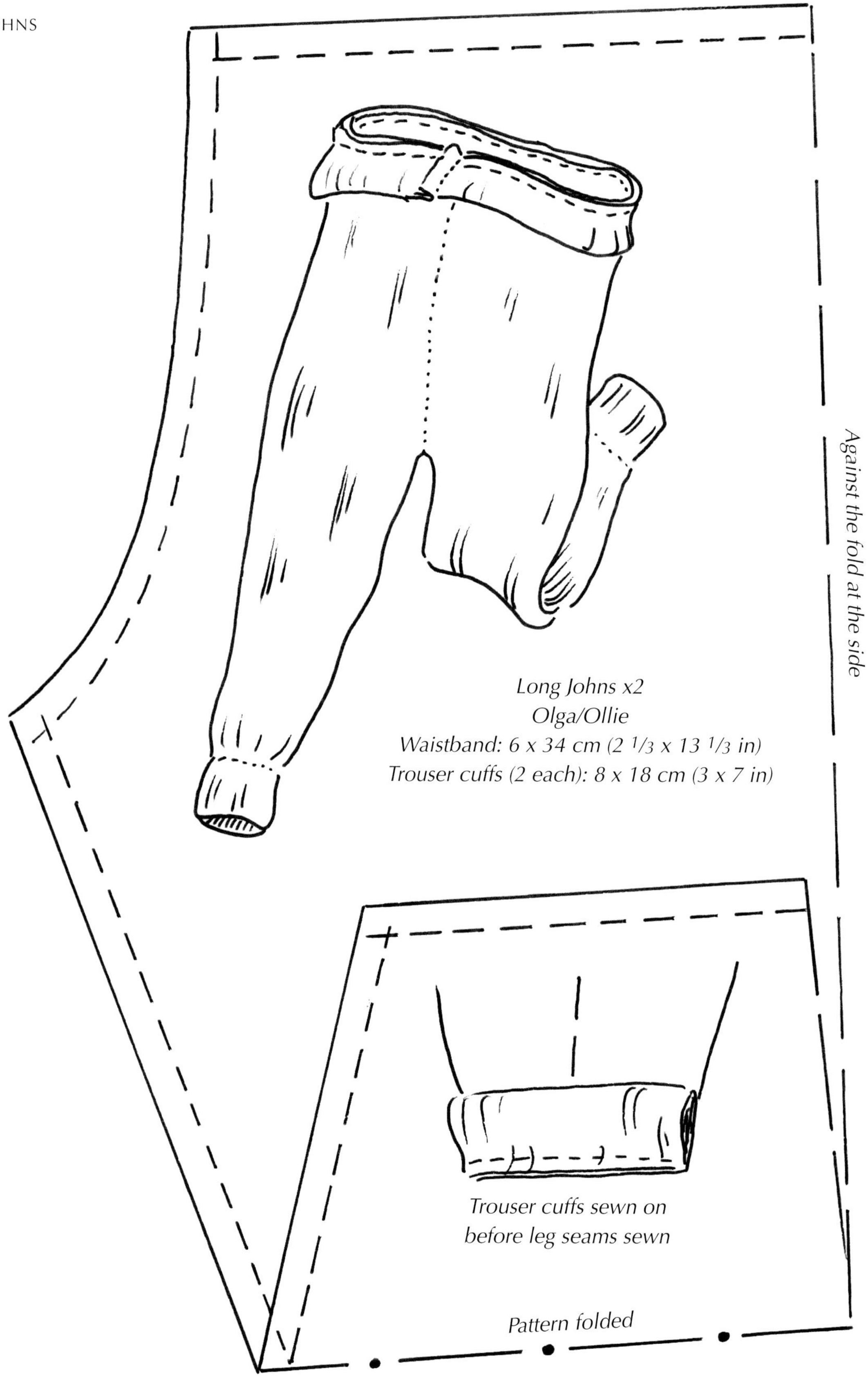

Against the fold at the side

Long Johns x2
Olga/Ollie
Waistband: 6 x 34 cm (2 $\frac{1}{3}$ x 13 $\frac{1}{3}$ in)
Trouser cuffs (2 each): 8 x 18 cm (3 x 7 in)

Trouser cuffs sewn on
before leg seams sewn

Pattern folded

82

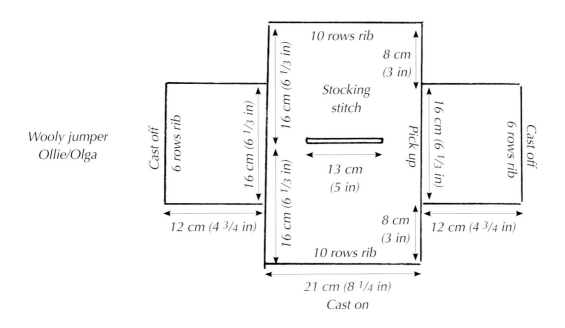

*Wooly jumper
Ollie/Olga*

10 rows rib

8 cm
(3 in)

16 cm (6 ⅓ in)

Stocking
stitch

16 cm (6 ⅓ in)

Cast off

6 rows rib

16 cm (6 ⅓ in)

Pick up

16 cm (6 ⅓ in)

Cast off

6 rows rib

13 cm
(5 in)

16 cm (6 ⅓ in)

8 cm
(3 in)

12 cm (4 ¾ in)

10 rows rib

12 cm (4 ¾ in)

21 cm (8 ¼ in)

Cast on

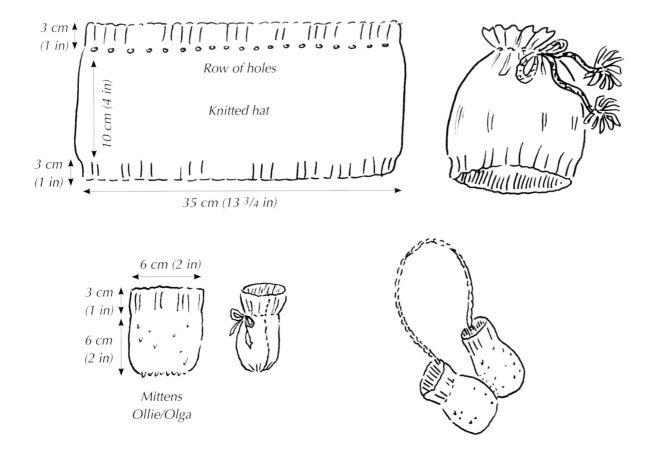

3 cm
(1 in)

Row of holes

Knitted hat

10 cm (4 in)

3 cm
(1 in)

35 cm (13 ¾ in)

6 cm (2 in)

3 cm
(1 in)

6 cm
(2 in)

*Mittens
Ollie/Olga*

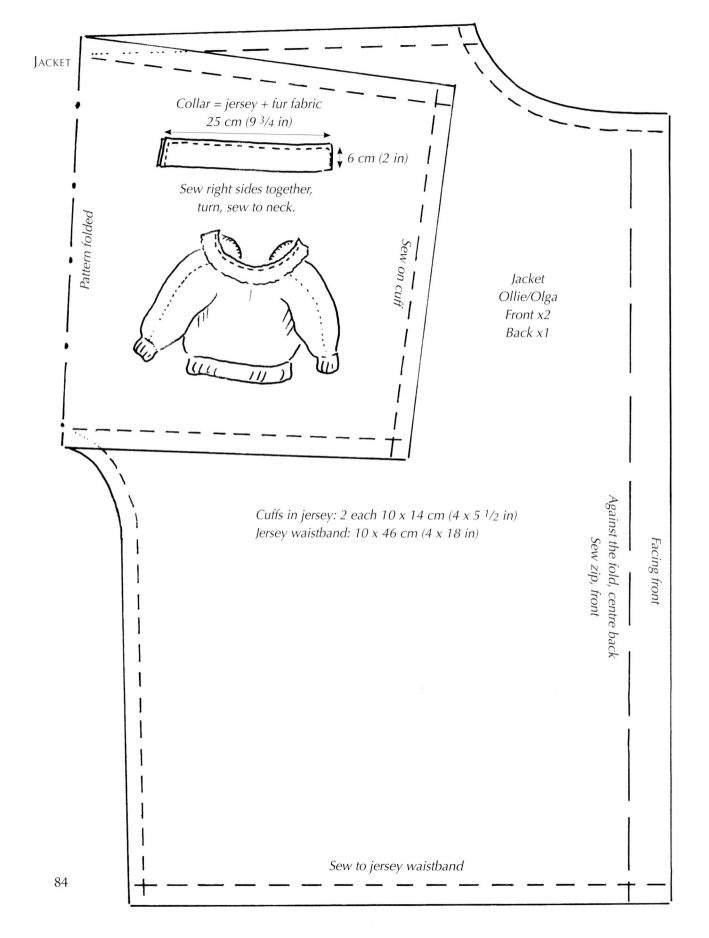

Collar = jersey + fur fabric
25 cm (9 ¾ in)

6 cm (2 in)

Sew right sides together,
turn, sew to neck.

Pattern folded

Sew on cuff

Jacket
Ollie/Olga
Front x2
Back x1

Cuffs in jersey: 2 each 10 x 14 cm (4 x 5 ½ in)
Jersey waistband: 10 x 46 cm (4 x 18 in)

Against the fold, centre back
Sew zip, front

Facing front

Sew to jersey waistband

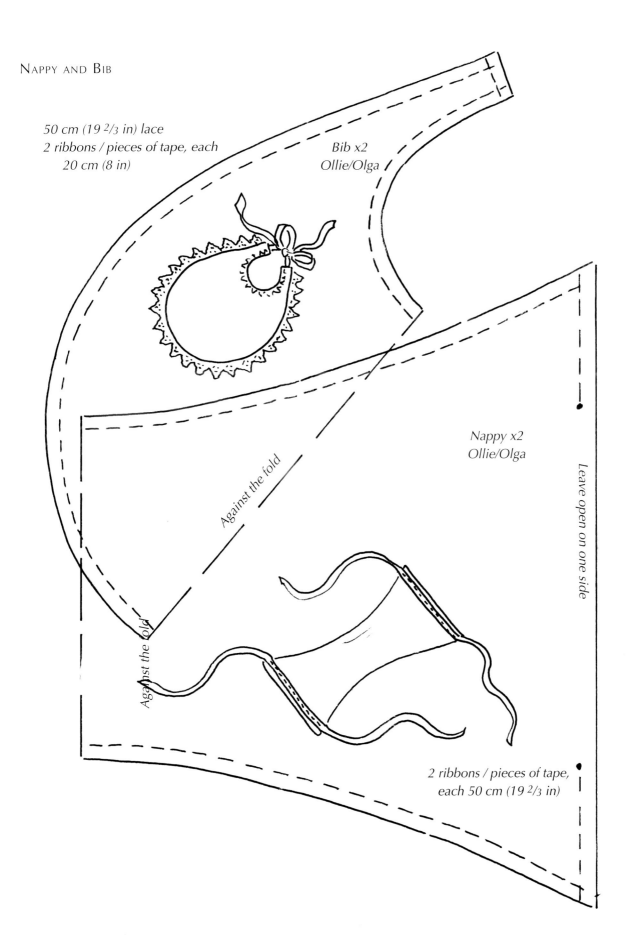

50 cm (19 $^2/_3$ in) lace
2 ribbons / pieces of tape, each
20 cm (8 in)

Bib x2
Ollie/Olga

Against the fold

Against the fold

Nappy x2
Ollie/Olga

Leave open on one side

2 ribbons / pieces of tape,
each 50 cm (19 $^2/_3$ in)

Max & Minnie

Max and Minnie are about 24 cm (9 1/2 in) tall. They have moveable arms and legs and are fun for slightly older children to play with. You can make a potty from Cernit (polymer) clay and tuck the doll into bed in a small box.

MATERIALS

- Flesh-coloured, thin cotton knit, folded double along the rib: 25 x 20 cm (10 x 8 in)
- Gauze tubing: 25 cm (10 in), 3–4 cm (1–1 1/2 in) wide
- Chopstick or other stick to turn the fabric and aid stuffing
- Stuffing wool: about 50 g (1 3/4 oz)
- A little wool for the hair
- Embroidery thread or buttonhole silk for the eyes and pink sewing thread for the mouth
- Flesh-coloured sewing thread and sewing thread to match the hair
- Strong thread for shaping the head
- 4 small round pieces of fabric or leather for 'buttons'
- A long darning needle
- Preferably a felting needle (medium) and a sponge to rest on

1. Trace the pattern pieces, cut them out and lay on to double fabric and draw round. Position the arms and legs vertically with the arrow following the direction of the rib. Lay the head/body piece along the folded edge of the fabric (figure 1).

2. Sew before you cut out the pieces! (Sew by hand with backstitch, or on a machine using stretch seam). Follow the dotted line to allow for 0.4 cm (1/6 in) seam allowance. Leave an opening at the top of the back of the arms and legs and at the top of the head/body piece. Cut the pieces out. Cut small nicks in the seam allowance around the thumb and over the foot. Turn the pieces right side out using the stick. Rub the fabric from the right side to bring the thumbs out.

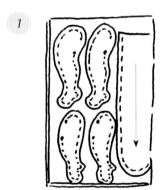

Well done, soon you'll be out of nappies, Max! Minnie stands next to him, offering encouragement. She is wearing her pyjamas, which you'll find on page 93. The potty is made of baked Cernit (polymer) clay.

3. Fold a thick length of wool to be 12 cm (4 3/4 in) long. Bind it tightly with thin strips of wool to make a backbone (a felting needle will help, resting on the sponge (figure 2).

4. At one end bind a hard, small ball made from very thin wool strips, to be the head. Ensure the wool is wrapped in different directions around the head. Add extra wool for the chin, cheeks and back of the head. The circumference of the head should be about 18 cm (7 in). In the same way build a body around the backbone. Using the felting needle you can shape the body, giving it a bottom and protruding tummy (figure 3).

5. Make a bag from gauze tubing by tying one end and turning inside out. Pull the tube over the head and down over the body. Cut off overlapping tubing and sew the ends together. Tie a strong thread around the neck. Thread a darning needle, long enough to go through the head, with strong thread. Shape the head (figure 4). This was described earlier in detail for Ellie and Emma, pages 27–29.

6. Pull on the fabric casing from the bottom and upwards so that the opening reaches the crown of the head. Make sure the seam is always at the centre back. Pull the fabric slightly, cut away any excess fabric, fold the

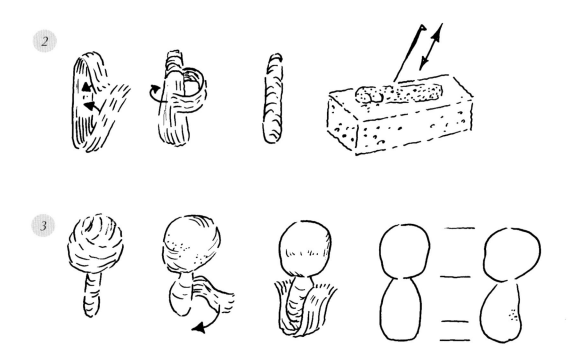

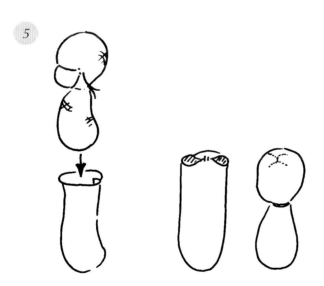

fabric neatly on top of the head and sew together by hand. Then using a needle and strong thread, wind the thread around the neck, sewing it securely in place, so that the fabric is pulled in (figure 5).

7. Arms and legs: first stuff a little wool into the hands and feet. Then form two matching arms and legs with wool stuffing. Begin as with the backbone with a length of wool around which you wind strips of wool very

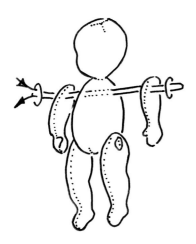

tightly (using a felting needle to help). Make the limbs thicker at the top. Add thin layers of wool to the arms and legs until they are equally thick and feel solid. Insert them into their fabric cases and sew the openings.

8. Cut four 'buttons' of leather (or fabric). Thread strong thread through a needle that is long enough to go through the whole body. Stick the needle through a button, on through the upper arm at the cross mark, then through the body at the cross, out

Max and Minnie are small dolls with moveable limbs and are easy to make. The head and body are fixed together, and the arms and legs attached with strong thread pulled tightly. On the left, you can see Max completed; to the right is a doll that's about to have its arms and legs attached. Small buttons of leather or fabric are positioned outside the arms and legs to protect the fabric from wear.

the other side, through the other arm and through a second button. Then turn and go back through the button, body parts and the first button. Pull the thread tightly so that the arms lie close to the body. Tie the ends of the threads together with several knots. Cut off the ends.

9. Attach the legs with buttons, in the same way as the arms, above.

10. Face markings. Minnie's eyes are sewn in linen thread. She has a happy mouth embroidered in small, slanting stitches of sewing thread (figure 7). Max's eyes are sewn in pearl cotton and his mouth is a made by a few parallel lines stitched in sewing thread (figure 8).

Minnie's hair

Minnie has small, thin plaits. Cover the head with stitches in two-ply, wool warp yarn or other very fine, strong yarn. Arrange the stitches like sun-rays coming from the centre of each plait. Leave long loose ends there and attach more lengths in the same place until the plaits are thick enough. Stitch covering stitches towards the hairline, leaving loose ends to form a thin fringe (figure 9).

Max's hair

Max has a covering layer of mohair wool on his head. Wind the yarn around your fingers so that you have equal lengths that will reach from the fringe to the nape of the neck. Lay the hair over the crown and sew it in place with several horizontal rows of stitching (figure 10).

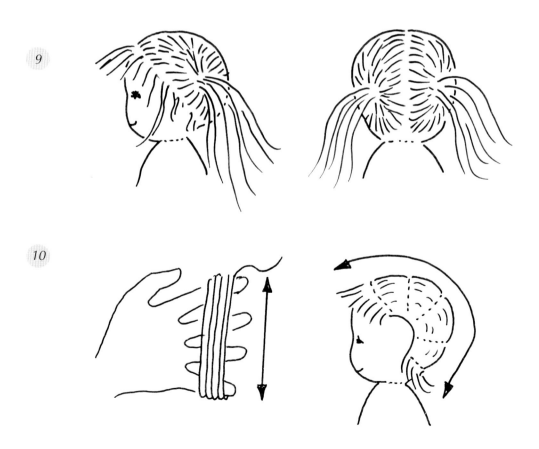

9

10

91

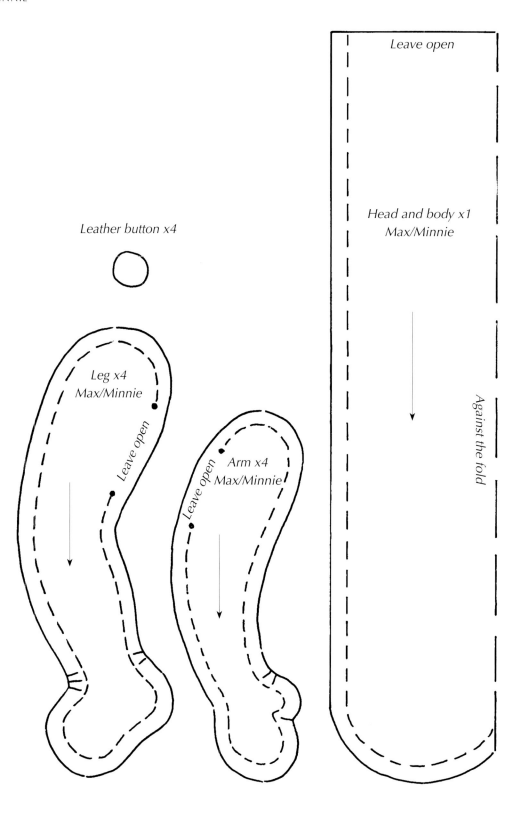

Leather button x4

Leg x4
Max/Minnie

Leave open

Arm x4
Max/Minnie

Leave open

Leave open

Head and body x1
Max/Minnie

Against the fold

Max and Minnie's clothes

Pyjamas

1. Cut out pieces from thin cotton jersey or cotton, following the pattern on page 95.
2. Turn under and sew the sleeve hems. Thread elastic through, pull until it's the right size then sew the ends in place.
3. Sew the arm and side seams.
4. Turn under and sew the leg hems. Thread elastic through, pull until it fits and sew the ends in place.
5. Sew the inside leg seams.
6. Zigzag around the neck and opening, turn in and sew down the hem allowance, or sew on an edging or trim.
7. Attach ribbons or a button and loop.

Nightcap

1. Cut out using the same material as the pyjamas
2. Sew the side seam.
3. Turn under and sew a double seam for the elastic at the bottom. Thread elastic through.
4. Run a row of gathering stitches along the upper edge and pull to gather.
5. Sew a woollen tassel on the top.

NIGHTCAP

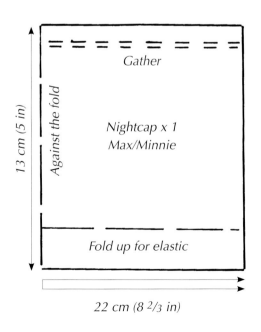

Gather

Against the fold

13 cm (5 in)

Nightcap x 1
Max/Minnie

Fold up for elastic

22 cm (8 2/3 in)

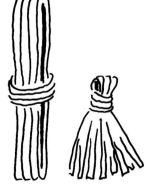

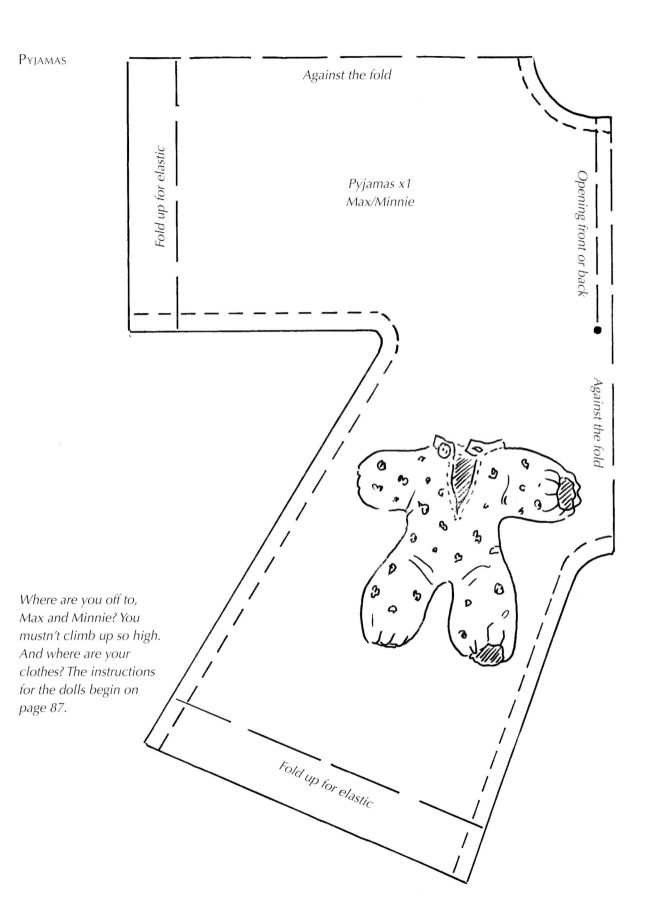

Against the fold

Fold up for elastic

Pyjamas x1
Max/Minnie

Opening front or back

Against the fold

Fold up for elastic

*Where are you off to,
Max and Minnie? You
mustn't climb up so high.
And where are your
clothes? The instructions
for the dolls begin on
page 87.*

Tim & Tina

Make your own Barbie doll with moveable arms and legs, sewn in stiff cotton fabric. Tim and Tina are almost 30 cm (12 in) tall.

MATERIALS
- Stiff flesh-coloured cotton fabric: 50 x 32 cm (19 2/3 x 12 1/2 in)
- Wool stuffing, about 10 g (1/3 oz)
- Sewing thread for the body, hair, eyes and mouth
- A little yarn for the hair, preferably thin, two-ply wool warp
- Chopstick or plant stick for turning material and stuffing
- Strong thread (such as rug warp) to secure arms and legs
- 4 small round pieces of leather or 4 buttons with large holes
- Darning needle, at least 7 cm (2 3/4 in) long
- Pliers for pulling the needle through

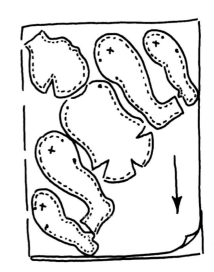

1. Trace the pattern pieces and transfer to double cotton fabric. Lay the pieces diagonally to the grain of the fabric (figure 1). Cut out the pieces.
2. Sew the head darts and the three smaller darts at the bottom of the body. Pin and sew all pieces with stretch setting following the dotted line. Trim the seam allowance. Cut small nicks in the seam allowance as indicated on

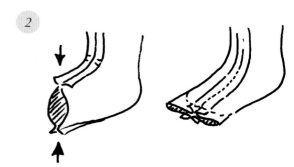

the pattern. Pinch the feet together seam to seam and sew a rounded seam across the lower edge (figure 2). Turn all pieces right side out.

How lovely to pick berries! For Tim and Tina the wild strawberries are almost as big as apples. Tim and Tina are made with moveable arms and legs. You can find the instructions for their clothes on pages 105–106.

3. Stuff all the pieces with plenty of wool, with the help of the stick. Shape the pieces as you stuff them, paying special attention to the cheeks and chin. Try not to put too much stuffing in the nose — it can look ugly. Fill the doll's bottom and stomach carefully. If the seam on the forehead wrinkles, you can make a small pleat above the hairline, pulling the seam straight. Sew the openings of the arms and legs. When the head and neck are well filled, sew a couple of stitches under the throat so that the wool stays in place.

4. Make room for the neck in the body. Attach the head to the body, turning in the body fabric's seam allowance and pinning front and back (figure 3). With small neat stitches, sew the body fabric to the head, around the neck. Use the stick to push a little more stuffing into the shoulders. Then sew the shoulder seams together.

5. Cut four 'buttons' of leather (or use real buttons, although these are not suitable for young children, should the buttons come loose). Thread a needle long enough to go right through the body with strong thread. Stick the needle through a button, on through the upper arm at the cross mark, through the body at the cross and out the other side, through the second arm, out through the button, and finally turn and go back through button, arm, body, arm and button (figure 4).

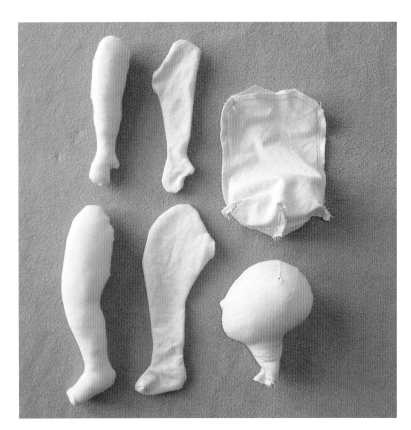

This is what the pieces for Tim and Tina look like sewn in normal cotton fabric.

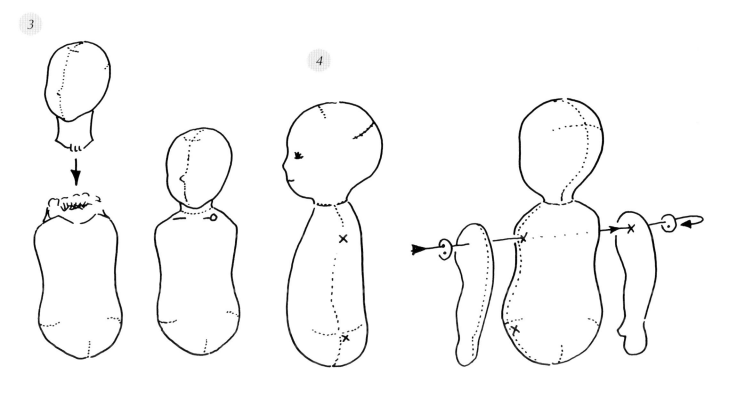

3

4

6. Pull the thread tight enough so that the arms lie close beside the body. Tie the threads together with several knots. Cut off the loose ends.
7. Secure the legs with buttons in the same way as the arms.
8. Sew the eyes as two pointed triangles, bases facing. Tim has a pupil drawn on his eyes in pencil. Tina has several vertical stitches in the centre of her eye (figure 5).
9. Sew the mouth with a few horizontal stitches in pink sewing thread.

5

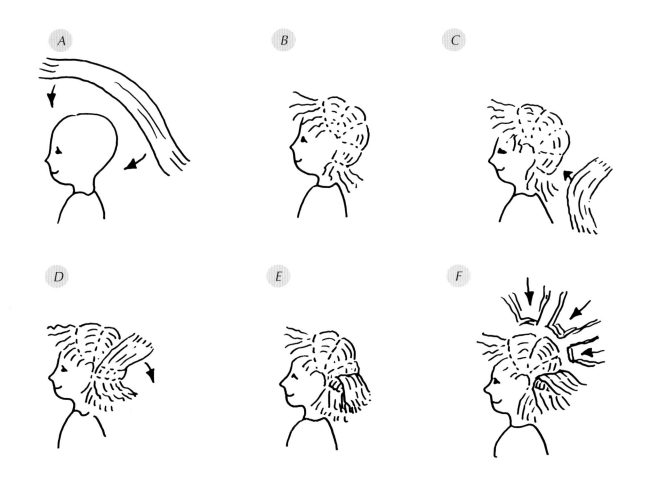

Tim's hair

Tim has tousled hair made from single-ply wool yarn. First lay a thin covering layer of parallel lengths over the head, including a fringe (A). Sew several horizontal seams with thread the same colour as the hair, the first at the hairline at the front and the last at the nape of the neck (B). Add more hair in the same way at the sides until it reaches the point where the ear would be.

Cut yarn double the hair length (C). Sew the hair in place with one seam a short way up from the nape. Sew another seam over the new hair but 1–2 cm ($^{1}/_{3}$–$^{3}/_{4}$ in) higher up (D). Fold back the new layer of hair (E). Continue with more hair layers, right up over the crown and forward to the fringe (F). You can also sew Tim's hair in the same way as Ollie's (see page 67).

Tina's hair

Tina has long hair made from strong two-ply wool warp yarn in two shades of brown. Cut yarn long enough to hang down on both sides of the head, as long as you like (A). Sew it in place along a centre parting, using thread the same colour as the hair. Spread the hair over the back of the head so that it also covers the neck (B). Sew several horizontal seams, including one from the hairline at the ears and one at the nape of the neck (C). Cut lengths of hair double the required length and follow the same method as for Tim, sewing the hair in place with two seams, one above the other, a couple of centimetres apart, around the head (D). Finally lay a layer of hair over the head again (E), but this time sew it in place only at the centre parting and with one seam on either side (F).

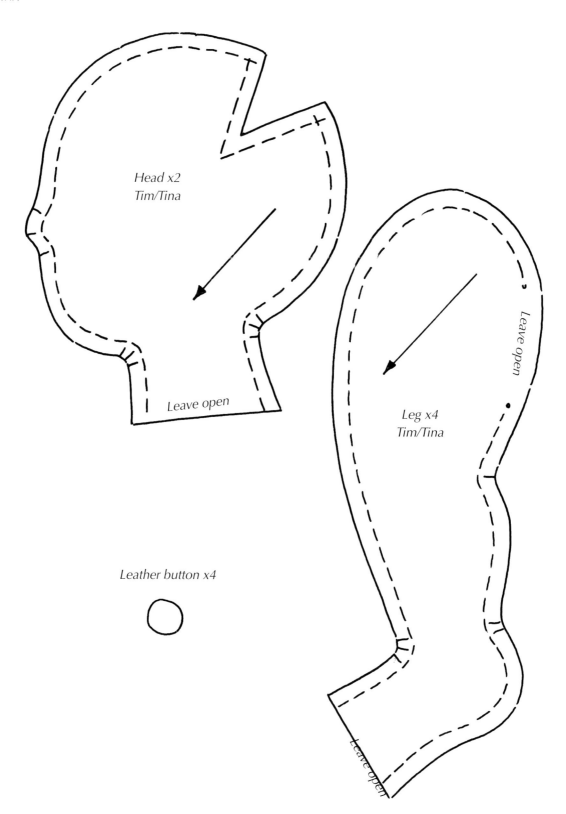

Head x2
Tim/Tina

Leave open

Leg x4
Tim/Tina

Leave open

Leave open

Leather button x4

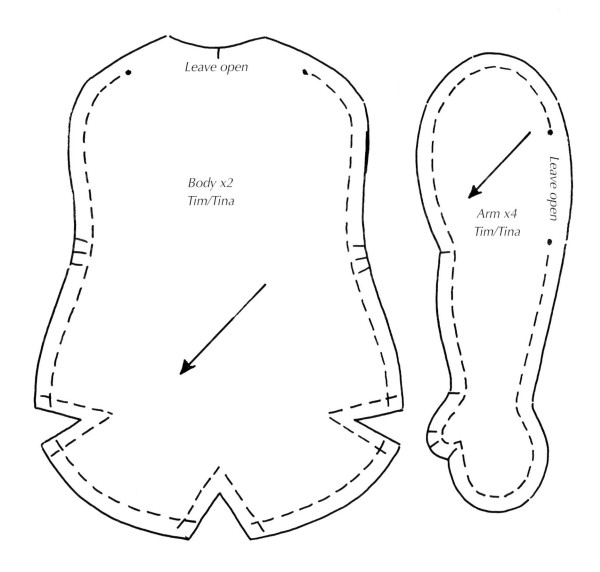

Leave open

Body x2
Tim/Tina

Arm x4
Tim/Tina

Leave open

TIM

TINA

Tim and Tina's clothes

Hooded sweatshirt

1. Cut out the pieces from soft jersey fabric, following the pattern on page 107.
2. Fold the cuffs double, right sides out. Place cuffs against the sleeve edges, sewing them right sides together.
3. Sew the sleeve and side seams.
4. Sew the hood seam.
5. Sew the hood to the neck, A to A.
6. Turn under and sew the front edge of the hood and the opening at the centre front of the sweatshirt.
7. Sew the small triangular insert, cut from a different-coloured fabric, into the bottom of the front opening.
8. Attach two ties to the front of the hood.

Bag

1. Cut out two identical rectangles in felt following the pattern on page 107.
2. Sew them to make a bag (do not turn the bag right side out).
3. Zigzag the edges.
4. Tack yarn around the opening, leaving long loose ends, which are tied together to become the shoulder strap.

Waistcoat

1. Cut out pieces in cotton fabric following the pattern on page 108.
2. Sew the side seams and the shoulder seams.
3. Zigzag all edges.

Long trousers

1. Cut out all the pieces in thin cotton material following the pattern on page 108.
2. Turn under the trouser hem and sew.
3. Sew the inside leg seams.
4. Sew the centre back and front seams.
5. Fold the waistband over, right sides facing, and sew in place around the waist.
6. Fold some of the pocket over to form a flap, sew the pocket to one trouser leg and then sew a button on the pocket.

Dress

1. Cut out the dress in cotton fabric following the pattern on page 109.
2. Turn under and sew the sleeve hems.
3. Sew the side and sleeve seams as one. Leave a small opening at the lower end.
4. Sew the lower hem, sewing in the seam allowance around the opening.
5. Zigzag around the neck.
6. Sew on lace at the bottom.

Tim and Tina are going to a midsummer garden party. They are each carrying a bag of spare clothes and have brought their felted dog (keeshond) along for company.

Panties

1. Cut out the pieces in thin cotton-jersey fabric following the pattern on page 109.
2. Sew the side seams.
3. Turn under and sew the leg hems. You may want to insert elastic in the hem, in which case pull the elastic and fasten on each side.
4. Sew the inside leg seams.
5. Fold the waistband under, place elastic against the fabric and stretch the elastic as you sew it to the fabric with straight seam.

Vest

1. Cut out the pieces in thin jersey fabric following the pattern on page 110.
2. Sew the side seams.
3. Zigzag around the neck, armholes and lower edge.

Fur fabric waistcoat

1. Cut out the pieces in fur fabric following the pattern on page 110.
2. Sew the shoulder seams.
3. Sew the side seams.
4. Sew on a button and loop.

Socks

1. Cut out the pieces in thin jersey fabric following the pattern on page 110.
2. Sew them together according to the pattern.
3. You can also use gauze tubing. Tie it at the bottom, turn and the sock is finished!

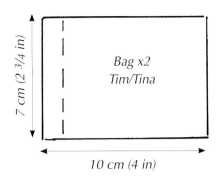

Bag x2
Tim/Tina

7 cm (2 ¾ in)

10 cm (4 in)

Cuffs: 2 x 7 cm (2 ¾ in)
Ties: 2 x 10 cm (4 in)

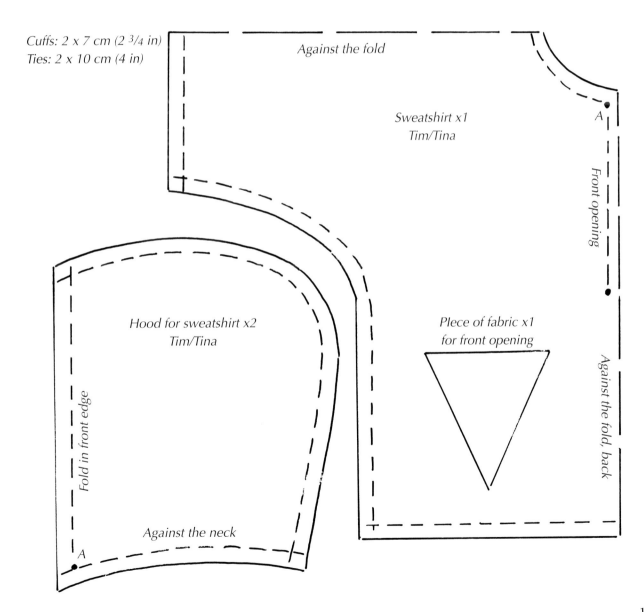

Against the fold

Sweatshirt x1
Tim/Tina

A

Front opening

Against the fold, back

Hood for sweatshirt x2
Tim/Tina

Piece of fabric x1
for front opening

Fold in front edge

Against the neck

A

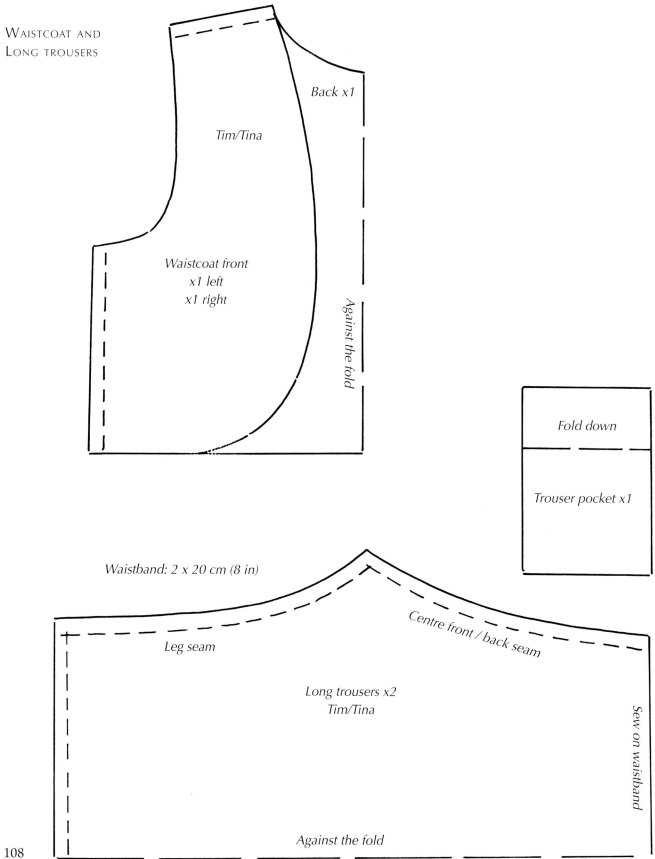

Tim/Tina

Back x1

Waistcoat front
x1 left
x1 right

Against the fold

Fold down

Trouser pocket x1

Waistband: 2 x 20 cm (8 in)

Leg seam

Centre front / back seam

Long trousers x2
Tim/Tina

Sew on waistband

Against the fold

108

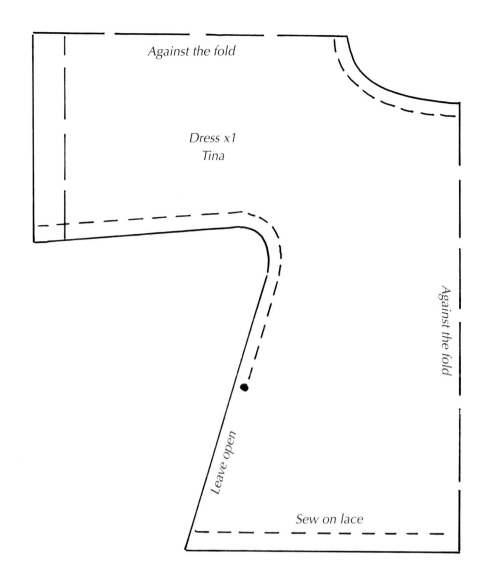

Against the fold

Dress x1
Tina

Against the fold

Leave open

Sew on lace

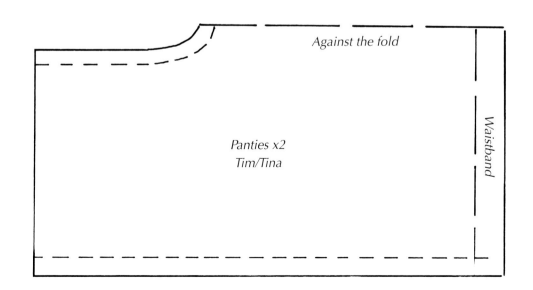

Against the fold

Waistband

Panties x2
Tim/Tina

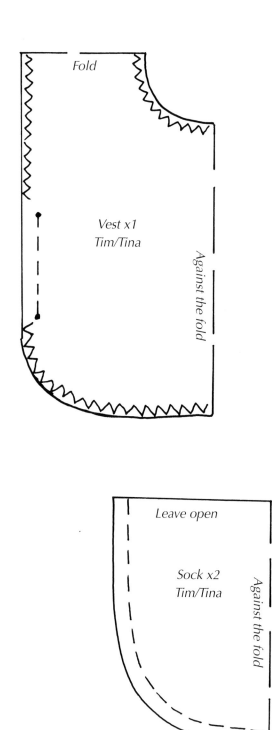

Fold

Vest x1
Tim/Tina

Against the fold

Leave open

Sock x2
Tim/Tina

Against the fold

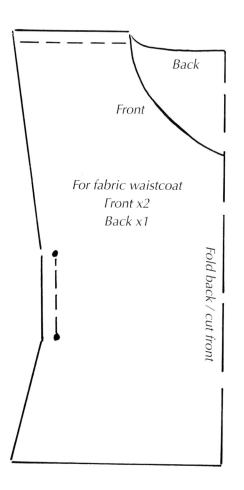

Back

Front

For fabric waistcoat
Front x2
Back x1

Fold back / cut front

The Nature Corner

Celebrating the year's cycle with seasonal tableaux

M. van Leeuwen and J. Moeskops

Seasonal nature tables are an invaluable way of making young children aware of the changing cycle of the year. With simple materials a series of colourful and effective tableaux can be made at home or in school.

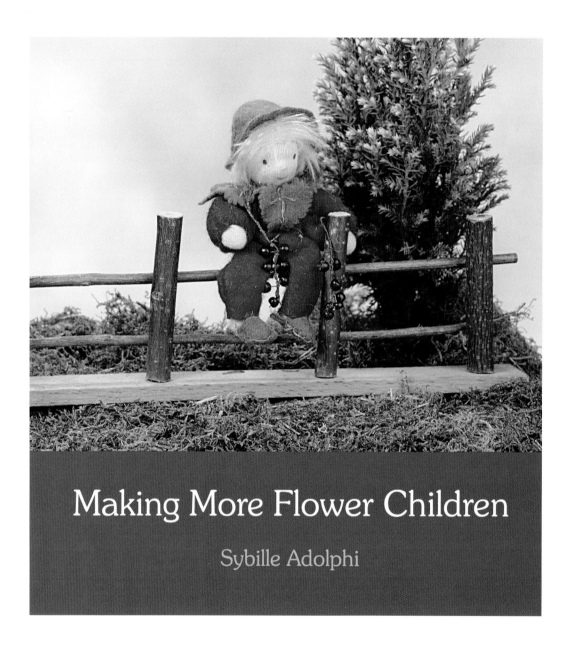

Making More Flower Children

Sybille Adolphi

This book contains all the patterns and instructions you will need to make your own flower children, and is clearly illustrated with diagrams and photographs throughout. Also available by the same author: *Making Flower Children*.